A Prince in the Queen City

The Life of Henry Mack

A Prince in the Queen City
The Life of Henry Mack

Michael W. Rich

Apprentice House Press
Loyola University Maryland

Copyright © 2019 by **Michael Rich**

All rights reserved. No part of this book may be reproduced or transmitted in any form or by any means, electronic or mechanical, including photocopy, recording, or any information storage and retrieval system, without prior permission from the publisher (except by reviewers who may quote brief passages).

First Edition

Paperback ISBN: 978-1-62720-190-2
Ebook ISBN: 978-1-62720-191-9

Printed in the United States of America

Design by Apprentice House
Marketing by Taylor Fluehr
Development by Hayley Morris

Published by Apprentice House

Apprentice House
Loyola University Maryland
4501 N. Charles Street
Baltimore, MD 21210
410.617.5265 • 410.617.2198 (fax)
www.ApprenticeHouse.com
info@ApprenticeHouse.com

To my family, both past and present.

Contents

Who was Henry Mack? 1
Family Origins 3
Early Years in Germany 5
Business Success in Cincinnati 9
Conflict, Contracts, and Controversy 15
Mack, Stadler & Co 21
Embroiled with the Grants 25
Contributions to Reform Judaism 29
The Foreman 37
Local Politics 41
When Ohio Dried Out 49
The Promise 55
The Chattanooga Choo Choo 59
Private Life 65
The Mack Family in America 75
Henry Mack's Relevance 79
Notes 81
About the Author 99

Who was Henry Mack?

Since his death more than a century ago, his name has faded into obscurity. Dusty tomes mention his name in passing. His face stares out from unlabeled photographs in archival files. And yet during his lifetime, he was an important figure in American Judaism. The national press described him as "one of the most prominent Hebrews in the country."[1] A local columnist ranked him as the most influential Jew in Cincinnati's political sphere of the second half of the nineteenth century.[2] He participated in, and often catalyzed many of the events that touched Jewish lives of his day.

By all traditional measures, his life was a success. His achievements were all the more remarkable because of all the hurdles he had to overcome. As the first of his clan to immigrate to the United States, he had no family to help him adjust to his new life. He stepped onto American soil with little money, a rudimentary education, and unable to speak the language. Adding to the challenge was that he was forced to make headway against the pervasive anti-Semitism of that era. His climb was made possible only through ambition, determination, and sheer effort.

Financial acumen earned him a fortune as a clothing merchant. That financial independence afforded him the time to become a public servant. First he joined forces with Rabbi Isaac Mayer Wise to create the infrastructure of the American Jewish Reform Movement. During his single term as a Cincinnati city councilman, he helped guide the city into the modern world. The foundations of Cincinnati's sewage system, garbage disposal, and public transportation could all be traced back to Henry Mack. His long tenure on the school board was highlighted by the nation's landmark First Amendment case that outlawed the reading of the Bible in the public schools. As a trustee of the Cincinnati Southern Railway, he was crucial in assuring the financial solvency of the country's first municipally owned railroad. His political career concluded as a state senator with him becoming the face of the anti-Prohibition faction that was unable to stop Ohio from adopting Sunday laws.

He rubbed elbows with several future U.S. presidents. He purposely affected two presidential elections and inadvertently influenced two others. He would reach the cusp of history when he came within one broken promise of becoming the first Jew to serve in a presidential cabinet.

In spite of all these positive contributions, his name was also associated with two less noble events. In the early months of the Civil War, civilian contractors were suspected of overcharging the military for poor quality material and equipment. Because his firm was a principal supplier of uniforms to the Union, Mack was caught up in the large net of a congressional investigation. The investigation added the term "shoddy" to our lexicon and led to the creation of the False Claims Act. His firm's dubious business deal with the father of Ulysses Grant triggered the most infamous act of anti-Semitism in American history. Found innocent of illicit behavior in both circumstances, the negative publicity still dented his reputation for years.

At the same time, he was recognized for having the courage to speak his conscience even at the cost of personal gain. In spite of learning his first words of English at age nineteen, he developed such a command of the language that he became acclaimed for his eloquent public speaking. He was an ardent patriot, vocally defending the liberties afforded him by his citizenship. A streak of generosity led him to spearhead fundraising efforts for those less fortunate, irrespective of their race, religion, or nationality.

The following biographical sketch, I hope, will reveal why he should again be recognized as one of the important figures in nineteenth-century American Jewish history.

Family Origins

The Mack family traces its roots back to the old German kingdom of Bavaria. It was not until the Napoleonic Wars that German states required their Jewish citizens to adopt surnames.[3] Before surnames were adopted, a German-Jewish male was often identified by a given name to which was suffixed the given name of his father. Therefore, when the patriarch of the Mack clan was born in the town of Demmelsdorf during the middle of the eighteenth century, he was called Isaac Mannlein. When, in the year 1813, Bavaria required its Jewish residents to acquire family names, the peddler Isaac Mannlein chose the surname Mack. Isaac's son Moses Isaac Mack became a clothing peddler and married Esther, daughter of Lemel Wolfsheimer, from nearby Bamberg.[4]

During the latter half of the eighteenth century and first half of the next century, the number of Jews granted the status of *Schutz* (roughly equivalent to "protection" and allowing its holder to marry and own property) in a given Bavarian village was set at a fixed number. In order for a young man to acquire a *Schutz*, he had to wait for another male to transfer that status to him or inherit one from a deceased male. With limited permits available, marriage was delayed.[5] The average age for a Jewish groom and bride in Demmelsdorf at that time was approximately thirty years old and twenty-five years old respectively.[6] Moses and Esther were thirty-one and twenty years old when united.[7]

Early Years in Germany

It was to Moses and Esther that Heinrich (he was also given the Hebrew name Elkan) Mack was born on December 23, 1820. Demmelsdorf was linked to other Jewish towns by the *Judenweg* ("Jewish Path") that led Jewish cattle traders in northern Bavaria from one fair to the next.[8] The city of Bamberg was only an hour's journey from Demmelsdorf by horse. The Main River traversed the countryside and was likely a source of recreation for the Mack boys. In 1826, 151 of Demmelsdorf's 242 inhabitants were Jews.[9, 10] Most of the town was owned as a fief under the Counts of Giech. Fortunately, these overlords were relatively protective of their Jewish residents as exemplified in 1699 when Jews were given sanctuary in the Castle of Giech during local famine rioting.[11] Henry and his siblings grew up in the reactionary sociopolitical climate that followed Napoleon's defeat. The freedoms granted Jews during the reign of Napoleon were swiftly repealed, and nowhere were these winds of change stronger than in Bavaria.

Henry was likely born in the Mack family house identified as house #13 in the Jewish *Matrikel*, or register, of Demmelsdorf. Henry's father and grandfather before him were identified as heads of the household at that address. The Mack family shared the structure with the Ochs family.[12] Shared abodes were the norm for the town's Jews. Thirty-three of the thirty-five Jewish families shared homes, with one family living in the lower floor and the other in the upper floor.[13, 14] The crowding was the result of the municipal restriction that forbade its Jews from either buying a house from a Christian or from building more houses. As families grew, living space could only be increased by adding rooms or an additional floor, or by converting attics from storage space. Houses were passed down from father to son. The Mack floor must have been crowded because Moses and Esther had ten children—Harmon (born in 1814), Mannlein (1816), Abraham

(1818), Henry (1820), Martin (1823), Simon (1825), Seligmann (1828), David (born Daniel in 1831), Julius (1835), and finally Julie (1837).[15]

Although a distinct ghetto did not exist in Demmelsdorf, the Jewish households were loosely clustered along a stretch of road.[16]

Moses Mack's occupation would have kept him away from home for days to weeks at a time in order to attend the fairs at which he sold his wares.[17] Lifelong bonds of friendship were already forming during Henry's childhood. He and Louis Stix "vowed eternal friendship" in 1832.[18]

The village synagogue was constructed in 1748. A religious school was opened in 1827 and Henry would have likely attended as a supplement to his public schooling.[19] Demmelsdorf had an elementary school but children attending secondary school had to walk to the neighboring village of Scheslitz.[20] Jewish children were required to attend German public schools as part of the Bavarian government's effort to assimilate its Jews.[21] Public schools were of poor quality. Consequently, Henry's formal education was limited, though he would become a champion of education later in his life.

His education was sufficient enough to earn him, at age thirteen, the position of copyist for the local clerk of courts. At age sixteen, he was apprenticed to a confectioner, and he became a master of the trade two years later.[22] For generations, the predominant occupation of Bavarian Jews was trade, notably peddling and cattle. In 1821, an estimated ninety-six percent of Bavarian Jews earned their livings through petty trade.[23] In an effort to assimilate its Jews into Bavarian society, the government made a concerted effort to move Jews away from trade and into such occupations as the handicrafts. [24, 25] Thus, Moses Mack was a peddler whereas Henry was trained to become a candy maker.

Henry and his older brother, Abraham, decided to leave their birthplace for America. Though religious oppression likely played a part in their decision, economic oppression was the principal force driving the brothers and many other Bavarian Jews from their homeland. Economic depression gripped Central Europe, particularly southwestern Germany, during the 1830s.[26, 27]

Moreover, the German states created laws that clearly intended to keep Jews impoverished second-class citizens. Special taxes were levied on them. The odious *Schutz* status all but prohibited younger siblings from having their own homes or starting their own families. Henry's grandfather Isaac died in 1837. Some of his possessions were auctioned, and two years later his *Schutz* was naturally inherited by Henry's eldest brother, Harmon.[28] If Henry and Abraham, the second- and third-oldest Mack brothers, remained in Bavaria, they would be unable to start their own families for quite some time. With such sanctions in place, it is little wonder that most Jews entering the United States between 1830 and 1850 were Germans, typically from small towns in northern Bavaria, and were rarely first-born sons.[29, 30]

With their parents' consent, Henry and Abraham left Demmelsdorf on July 28, 1839. They made their way to Hamburg, 300 miles to the north, traveling the entire way on foot. They set sail from Hamburg on August 17 and arrived in New York City ten weeks later.[31] They may have met up with an old acquaintance from Demmelsdorf who was already living in New York. This was a common practice through which a "seasoned" immigrant helped his "greenhorn" townsmen to adjust to their adopted country. The Mack brothers, in turn, would later help another Demmelsdorf immigrant—their old friend Louis Stix.[32]

Business Success in Cincinnati

Unable to find employment in New York City, the brothers sold a pocket watch and a gold ring given to them by their parents and used the fifteen dollars from that sale to purchase goods for peddling through the countryside. By the spring of 1840, they had parlayed that fifteen dollars into $500. Henry proudly recalled one particular trip to Jewett City in Connecticut. While peddling, he came across a package lying on the railroad tracks. The package was addressed to "Rev. Mr. Ely, Jewett City." He personally delivered the parcel, which contained a silk dress and a twenty dollar bill. Mr. Ely acclaimed his honesty, gave him a monetary reward, and provided the added windfall of referrals to his friends and neighbors. Henry devoted the winter of 1839-40 to learning the language of his adopted homeland. He did so by comparing passages from an English Bible with passages from its German counterpart.[33]

Louis Stix arrived in the spring of 1841, and once reunited the three men decided to travel west to Cincinnati.[34] But why Cincinnati? Certainly the Macks were not alone in making the Queen City of the West their destination. Between 1840 and 1860, the Jewish population of Cincinnati surged from 1,000 to 7,500 persons, making it the largest concentration of "Israelites" west of the Atlantic Coast.[35]

Several factors attracted German Jews to Cincinnati. Most obvious were the economic opportunities that drew Jews and Gentiles alike to the American frontier.

Also, by 1840, a thriving German community already existed in Cincinnati. Nearly thirty percent of its citizens had been born in German states, an increase from a mere five percent a decade earlier. Six of the city's twenty nine periodicals were printed in German.[36] Cultural and linguistic barriers were therefore reduced.[37]

Cincinnati had already developed a reputation as a "sort of paradise for Hebrews" where Jews were more readily accepted economically and socially than in other communities.[38] Until this time, American Jews had huddled in a few major communities along the East Coast out of fear that the frontier would wrest from them their religious identity. But by 1840 a substantial, if not flourishing, Jewish community already existed, so that a Jewish Cincinnatian need not worry for lack of opportunity to remain pious.

As word of this "paradise" got back to Bavaria, a chain migration occurred. In Demmelsdorf, for example, at least thirty young males out of a total Jewish population of 136 made the trek to Cincinnati between 1830 and 1865.[39] Louis Stix's older brother Carl came to Cincinnati during the 1830s and Louis was likely moving to Cincinnati to join his brother.[40] Many of Demmelsdorf's Jewish émigrés would figure prominently in the history of Cincinnati; among their names were Mack, Stix, Stadler, Pritz, and Krauss. Once reacquainted in the New World, townsmen formed tight bonds that resulted in lifelong friendships (e.g., the Macks and Louis Stix), business partnerships (e.g., the Macks and Stadlers), and even marriages (e.g., the Macks and Stadlers). This band of Demmelsdorf men became so important in Cincinnati that one newspaper dubbed them the "aristocrats."[41]

The details of the trip from New York City to Cincinnati were recorded by Louis Stix in his memoirs. Abraham Mack took charge of the travel arrangements. The first leg of the journey, from New York to Albany, was made by Hudson River steamboat. Schenectady was reached next by railroad, and from there Buffalo by canal boat. Abraham had contracted with the canal boat captain to reach Buffalo in time to catch a steamboat to Cleveland. When they arrived too late, Abraham threatened to sue the canal boat captain for breach of contract. While awaiting the next boat to Cleveland, they learned that on August 9, 1841 the first boat had caught fire on Lake Erie and that most of its passengers had perished.[42] Of the 242 fatalities on the steamship *Erie*, most were recent immigrants to the New World.[43] In light of this "providential escape," the suit was dropped. Most of the remaining journey, from Cleveland to Cincinnati, was made by canal.[44]

Once in Cincinnati, Henry began peddling the countryside with a horse and wagon, while his brother opened a butcher shop. The following spring, Henry opened a general store at Monroe, Ohio. Having prospered in Monroe, he soon opened a second store at Felicity, Ohio.[45, 46]

Now in his mid-20s, Henry had blue eyes, a dark complexion, a "high" forehead (receding hairline) and brown hair. He had not yet grown the beard that would distinguish him in later years.[47] On November 1, 1844 he became a naturalized U.S. citizen.[48]

In 1845, he sold his Felicity store and had Abraham manage his Monroe store so that he could return as quickly as possible to Bavaria, where their mother was terminally ill.[49]

He later recalled the portion of this melancholy journey that took him from France to his native country. He rode from Paris to Frankfurt-am-Main via a diligence, a larger European version of the American stagecoach. Drawn by a team of horses, this early mode of transportation could accommodate upwards of ten passengers. His travelling companions in the carriage were former U.S. Congressman Ebenezer Jackson, Jr. and his family. Jackson spoke fluent French allowing him to translate for the passengers while in France. Once the vehicle crossed into Germany, Henry returned the favor. The two men passed much of their time swapping stories about their respective Masonic lodges.[50]

In Frankfurt, Henry parted ways with the Jacksons and checked into a hotel to recover from the rough ride. During his five days in Frankfurt, he attended a local Masonic lodge and enjoyed the company of its members. One of those Masons provided his American counterpart with a personal tour of the city.[51]

Esther Mack died in May, three weeks before her son could reach Demmelsdorf.[52] After spending several weeks in Germany reuniting with his mourning family, Henry returned to Ohio.[53]

His return to his Bavarian homestead did provide him with one fortunate circumstance. He met Rosalia Mack, who was unrelated, from the nearby hamlet of Altenkunstadt.[54] The following August, Rosalia arrived in New York City with several of her family members.[55] The clan immediately moved west to Cincinnati. On September 15, 1846, Rosalia and Henry were married in a boarding house at the corner of Fifth and Sycamore Streets by Rabbi Marschutz.[56, 57] They would have nine children: Isaac (born in 1847), Millie (1849), Harry (1851), Henrietta ("Yetta") (1853), Willie (1855), Emil (1857), Louisa (1860), Alfred (1862), and Theodore ("Tay") (1864). As was common in those times, not all of the Mack children survived into adulthood. Isaac died in the cholera outbreak of 1849 and Willie died ten years later.[58]

Henry now closed his Monroe store and opened the dry-goods store H.&A. Mack with Abraham in Cincinnati. Following his mother's death, the remainder of Henry's immediate family (brothers Harmon, Simon, Martin, David, and Julius, sister Julie, and father Moses) joined him in Cincinnati. In the spring of 1847, four of the brothers—Henry, Abraham, Harmon, and Simon—formed the clothing firm of Mack & Bros.[59, 60]

Early on, the firm foundered and nearly failed. Rather than declare bankruptcy, the four brothers increased their efforts and temporarily opened additional stores in Columbus and Dayton as outlets for selling their clothing.[61] Simon and Martin managed the Columbus store.[62] The business weathered the storm, with Henry once and for all taking the financial helm. By 1852, the credit-rating firm of Dun & Co. reported that the credit of Mack & Bros. was "rather better; have done well the past year... nearly doubled their capital in the last 2 years... large business worth 25 [thousand dollars]."[63]

Henry Mack's career was typical of the successful German-Jewish immigrants of that era. The immigrant began peddling through the countryside, perhaps acquiring a pushcart or a horse and wagon. With some luck and a great deal of hard work, a peddler might purchase a retail store in an outlying town, as Henry did in Monroe and Felicity. With further success, he might go beyond retailing to become a wholesaler or manufacturer in a city, as Henry did in Cincinnati.[64, 65]

His career was also typical in his entrance into the manufacture and sale of ready-made men's apparel. By 1860, more than half of Cincinnati's Jewish populace was employed in the clothing industry. Sixty-five of the city's seventy wholesale clothing firms were owned by Jews.[66, 67]

Prior to mid-century, commercially available clothing was custom fitted to an individual and then hand-stitched by a seamstress or tailor. This centuries-old tradition was carried out in the seamstress's home or tailor's shop. The invention of the sewing machine and demand for uniforms during the American Civil War would transform this cottage industry into one of the most important sectors of the economy.[68] The Mack brothers' timing was impeccable. After entering this trade on the cusp of industrialization, they would ride the wave to personal success.

During the 1850s, Isaac Singer began to manufacture the first practical sewing machines, allowing for mass production of clothing. Production of ready-made clothing shifted into large workshops in which dozens of laborers toiled over sewing machines. Much of the work was still contracted out to seamstresses who sewed fabrics into garments by hand in their homes. These workshops would evolve over ensuing decades into the sweatshops that would fill muckraking stories and drive unionization in the Progressive Era.[69]

The Civil War accelerated this process by creating the sudden need for millions of uniforms. Manufacturers responded by creating a limited selection of uniform sizes and bringing all workers together under one roof. When peacetime came, these standard sizes and clothing factories were converted to the production of civilian clothing.[70]

As ready-made clothing became increasingly affordable to the masses, sales skyrocketed. The Queen City was propelled into a clothing manufacturing center. During the 1850s, clothing surpassed all of the city's other industries in terms of value. In 1851, nine hundred fifty shop workers and six thousand seamstresses made less than two million dollars worth in apparel. Just eight years later, seven thousand shop workers (using one thousand sewing machines) and seven thousand five hundred at-home seamstresses made fifteen million dollars worth in attire. From the eve of the war through the 1870s Cincinnati trailed only New York City in clothing production.[71]

The groundwork for Mack & Bros.' success had been laid. The 1856 entry in the Dun & Co. Reports found that the brothers, "incredible as it may seem… have now in monthly business upward of 90 thousand dollars." The entry goes on to describe the Macks as "all married; excellent character and fine habit; fine capacity; accounted perfectly honorable and are first rate credit here."[72]

Afflicted with tuberculosis, Abraham Mack quit the business in 1858, with plans to seek medical help and vacation in Europe with his family.[73, 74]

Abraham may have had a premonition. Or, perhaps, he flashed back to his near miss with the Lake Erie steam ship catastrophe of 1841. Long distance travel in that era carried considerable risk. Whatever the reasons, he updated his will using foreshadowing tones: "Inasmuch as I am about to take a sea voyage with my family and we are all in the hands of the Almighty, if it should be his will that none of my family should survive said voyage…"[75]

Three days after signing his will, Abraham, his wife, and their six children departed on the Cincinnati Express train to New York City. At 6:30 a.m. on May 12, 1858, the passenger train was riding over the Sauquoit Creek Bridge near Utica while another train was traveling over the bridge in the opposite direction. The combined weight of the two trains caused the bridge to collapse, resulting in the deaths of nine passengers and injury to another fifty-six. Two of Abraham's young children were amongst the dead.[76-78] Henry traveled to New York City to attend to his grieving loved ones. A month later, Henry wrote to *The New York Times* that the Mack family was grateful for the compassion and assistance provided his brother's family during their physical and emotional convalescence. He also noted that Abraham "was seriously and perhaps permanently injured."[79] Abraham survived the train wreck only to succumb to consumption three years later. He died on the Portuguese island of Madeira, frequented by consumptives because of its mild climate.[80-82]

Conflict, Contracts, and Controversy

As noted, the Civil War was a boon for the garment industry in general, but particularly so for the Mack brothers.

The nation plunged into bloodshed with the opening salvos fired upon Ft. Sumter on April 12, 1861. The Union's war machine began to mobilize quickly. The day after the Confederate flag was raised above the South Carolina fort, President Lincoln called for 75,000 volunteers. Three months later, in the wake of another federal loss at Bull Run, Congress authorized the raising of an additional 500,000 men. By the end of 1861, Ohio had spent more than a million dollars clothing its troops.[83]

Flush with patriotic fervor, volunteers poured into Columbus. Poorly prepared quartermasters were handed unprecedented amounts of money with the mandate of quickly feeding, clothing, and arming masses of soldiers. It was the ideal environment for profiteering. Soon cries of nepotism, bribery, and price gauging filled the air.[84]

Contractors across the North were accused of providing poor quality supplies. Early uniforms and blankets were manufactured from a material called shoddy. Shoddy was composed of scraps of wool that had been pieced together. This material tended to fall apart in the rain and under the duress of marching. The term "shoddy" soon came to represent all inferior military supplies and eventually entered the American lexicon as synonymous with any poorly made product.[85]

As reports of such unscrupulous behavior reached Washington, the House of Representatives created the Select Committee on Government Contracts. The committee crisscrossed the nation, investigating these claims of corruption. Government and military officials, as well as contractors and their representatives were interviewed. Their thousands of pages of testimony were presented to Congress.[86]

The most important and long-lasting outcome of these investigations was passage in March 1863 of the False Claims Act. The new law made defrauding the government illegal, punishable by jail time and heavy fines. Moreover, it included the whistleblower provision that encouraged private citizens to report fraud by rewarding them with a share of any recovered funds. More than 150 years later, the False Claims Act remains an important weapon in the Justice Department's armamentarium against corruption.[87]

While the Macks fared well financially and were not found guilty of any illegal activity, their reputations did not go unscathed.

Ohio Governor William Dennison awarded the state's first army clothing contract to Mack & Bros. One thousand uniforms were furnished at sixteen dollars apiece.[88] In keeping with the "spoils" system, large army contracts seemed to be disproportionately awarded to "party men." Henry was by now an influential and faithful Republican.[89] From April through July a series of contracts were made between Mack & Bros. and Ohio's quartermaster, Captain John Dickerson.

The clothiers manufactured so many uniforms early in the war that one periodical quipped that "the Union was marching off to war with the mark of Mack."[90] One war correspondent wrote that he was riding off to battle "armed against the rebels, with a revolver, and against the weather with two army shirts, and one of Mack & Bro's splendid overcoats."[91]

The Select Committee asked Dickerson why contracts did not always go to the lowest bidders. He explained that the urgency and scope of the crisis required the army to obtain supplies from whichever vendors could provide large quantities of high quality (i.e., regulation) goods quickly.[92]

By October 1861, three large Cincinnati clothing firms combined for the purpose of filling contracts with the U.S. Government. The conglomerate of Mack, Stadler & Glaser offered the economies of scale needed to fill massive orders quickly and cheaply.

The separate firms of Mack & Bros., Stadler & Bros., and Glaser & Bros. continued independently throughout the war to fulfill their private orders.

Uniting under one business aegis allowed the new mega-firm to share infrastructure. Glaser & Bros. already had a branch in Indianapolis, the headquarters of Indiana's quartermaster. By offering a common bid, the three avoided undercutting each other with competing bids.

Henry Mack estimated that by March 1862, the combined firm had filled $1.4 million in federal contracts.[93] Max Stadler placed their early profits at between ten and twelve percent.[94] During one four-month period in 1861, the firm manufactured nearly 200,000 articles of clothing.[95] In 1862, the clothiers received close to $1.3 million in government clothing contracts, making it the largest outfitter in Ohio and fourth largest in all of the Union that year.[96] The financial gains from this windfall ballooned the value of Mack & Bros. from $100,000 before the war to a postwar figure of $500,000![97]

By now, Henry was likely well-known in the greater Cincinnati area as demonstrated by the following anecdote. In 1861, there appeared in the Queen City a man who called himself Dr. Lewis Adolus. He claimed to have recently arrived from London where he served as the private tutor for the children of British Prime Minister Lord John Russell. Adolphus opened a school for boys in the affluent suburb of College Hill. Having convinced others of his honorable intentions, he began swindling dozens of victims out of money. His misdeeds in Ohio ended in late 1863 when he forged the name of "Henry Mack & Bros." onto at least $4,000 worth of promissory notes. By midway thru the Civil War, Henry's wealth and reputation must have been such that Adolphus had chosen to forge his signature. The premise of the scam would have been to use the Mack name recognition to fool victims into believing the veracity of the falsified notes. Upon being discovered but before he could be apprehended, the imposter fled to New York whence he sailed to Liverpool.[98]

The state of Henry's financial fortunes at the onset of the war was also displayed when he stepped in to aid his brother-in-law. Leonard W. Mack had been a partner in a coal business with Faust Freidenreich and J. G. Duerbeck. When Leonard decided to leave the company in 1860, his two partners tried to buy his share from the parent company of Springer, Freidenreich & Co. in Baltimore for $7,000 in promissory notes. When the parent company refused to endorse the notes, Henry did so. Charles Fries, an associate of Freidenreich and Duerbeck, had assured Henry that the pair had enough equity to cover the debts. Henry's personal wealth had become substantial enough to back such a sum at a time when the average American's annual income was a mere $297. Unfortunately for Henry, the pair could only repay $3,800 of the notes. In response, Henry sued Fries for remainder of the debt, plus $7,400 in accrued interest. He accused the defendant of knowingly misleading him. The jury of the Superior Court of Cincinnati sided with Henry, based largely upon "his character as a reliable business man and as a man of undoubted veracity." Fries appealed to the Ohio Supreme Court where, in 1877, the verdict was overturned based upon a legal loophole. This case, as we shall see later in this biographical sketch, would have ramifications during Henry's service as a trustee for the Cincinnati Southern Railway.[99-101]

The tremendous returns of the first twelve months of the war withered as 1862 progressed. The Macks, Stadlers, and Glasers found themselves on the defensive as jealous competitors accused them of dishonest dealings, often lacing their comments with anti-Semitic overtones. Government delays in payments forced the firm to borrow money with interest. Their profits were also eroded by greedy officials looking for their cuts.

Mack, Stadler & Glaser agents traveled to the quartermaster offices of Indiana's and Illinois's regiments in Indianapolis and St. Louis respectively. One Indiana clothier complained that it had been unfairly beaten by a higher bid from "some Jews in Cincinnati."[101] Indiana's quartermaster John H. Vajen countered that the Indiana manufacturers lost the bid because their uniforms were "flimsy" and that they had tried to bribe him. Vajen mirrored the comments of his Ohio counterpart Dickerson in justifying an occasional award to a higher bidder if they could deliver a large order of regulation items when needed promptly. For this reason, in one case he gave "some large firms in Cincinnati... contracts for two regiments instead of one." Vajen estimated that roughly one-third of the clothing and blankets worn by Indiana's forces were procured from Cincinnati, mostly from the three houses of Kuhn & Rinskoft, Heidelback, and Mack, Stadler & Glaser.[103]

As for the intimation of bribery, Vajen admitted that some suppliers "donated" goods and money to be directly distributed to troops in need. He specifically noted that Mack, Stadler & Glaser "donated" a bale of fifty blankets along with $300 intended for purchase of necessities for Indiana's soldiers.[104] Henry Mack corroborated that these were donations for troops rather than bribes to quartermasters or inspectors. He bristled at the notion that he would bribe an official – "I should have given the cold shoulder to any such proposition."[105]

Both Henry and his company's salesman William Kraus were queried about a report that the firm had given an Indiana statehouse official $200 to expedite processing of payment vouchers. Kraus indignantly responded that he turned down such requests from two individuals. It was only after he was unable to overcome the roadblocks put up by the military bureaucrats at the statehouse that he acquiesced to a request from a third person. Kraus denied that the $200 was a bribe but instead argued that he considered it a legitimate payment for an official service. He concluded that it had become the only means for conducting such business – "Many others paid money for a similar purpose."[106]

Mack testified to the Select Committee that upon learning of Kraus's action, he became livid. From a practical standpoint, he opposed such a payment because it cut into their profit margin. He also expressed frustration over the reason why his salesman felt the need to resort to such payments. The U.S. government's delays in payments financially hurt his firm. In March 1862, the federal government still owed the clothier $50,000 for shipments sent four months earlier. The delay forced him to borrow money at high interest rates. He thus painted himself as the actual victim: "We furnished goods… at a very low figure….We have lost money by furnishing the goods." He insinuated that the government should not be attacking him but rather looking at the situation in Indianapolis: "There was great rascality going on there."[107]

The Select Committee must have heard enough during their investigations to have a grand jury indict a number of Cincinnati firms for overcharging the federal government. The Macks, Stadlers, and Glasers were part of the round-up but were all found innocent of the charges.[108, 109]

As the war dragged on, military contracts shifted towards East Coast manufacturers, particularly those in Philadelphia and New York. Over the course of the Civil War, Mack, Stadler & Glaser filled a total of $1.788 million in federal contracts, more than any other Cincinnati clothier. But by the second half of 1862, seven hundred employees had to be laid off by Cincinnati's clothing industry as their military contracts dried up. Mack, Stadler & Glaser received only $163,000 in military orders in 1863 and none in 1864.[110, 111]

Author's note: For additional information about the role of Jewish clothing contractors in the Civil War, please read Adam D. Mendelsohn, <u>The Rag Race: How the Jews Sewed Their Way to Success in America and the British Empire</u> (New York: New York University Press, 2015).

Mack, Stadler and Company

With the close of the war, Mack, Stadler & Glaser dissolved. In 1866, brother Simon joined Glaser & Bros. to form Mack, Glaser & Co. clothiers in New York City. The remaining Mack partners, Henry and Harmon, then combined with Stadler & Bros. to form Mack, Stadler & Co. in 1868. As they must have discovered during the war, mergers allowed for economies of scale. During the nine months preceding the merger, the monthly sales for Mack & Bros. and Stadler & Bros. were $21,000 and $27,000 respectively. Over the next year, the new conglomerate grossed only $25,000 per month but then rebounded the following year to $44,000 per month. In comparison, Proctor & Gamble's monthly sales were only $32,000.[112-114]

A sign of their financial ascent was the move of Mack & Bros. from 78 West Pearl Street to the more affluent address of 109 West Third Street.[115, 116] Facing the new Mack, Stadler & Co. storefront was the nationally renowned luxury hotel known as The Burnet House.[117] Contemporaries described Third Street as "the most important business street in the city." It was lined with many of Cincinnati's wealthiest banking, realty, insurance, and clothing firms.[118] The Third & Fourth Street horsecar line passed in front of the Mack establishment. These horsecars resembled later electric streetcars in that they served as public transportation on rail tracks. Unlike electric streetcars, however, these cars were pulled by horses.[119]

Henry and Harmon were "each considered wealthy," and their new firm was "one of the leading houses" in the clothing industry.[120] In 1860, Henry was living in Cincinnati's Second Ward and his real estate was valued at $25,000 in addition to $10,000 in other equity.[121] In 1862, he purchased a new house for his family in the adjacent Sixteenth Ward from Mr. Henry Pace for $16,000.[122] He soon also purchased a summer home in Mt. Airy, a suburb northwest of the city. By 1870, Henry reported his real estate worth to be $130,000 and his personal estate to be worth an additional $125,000.[123]

Cincinnati had become the Midwest's ready-made clothing hub. Between 1860 and 1869, the number of Cincinnatians employed in the industry rose from 789 to 1,907 while the value of their product increased from $7,400,000 to more than $16,000,000. In the latter year, the city hosted an International Exposition of Textile Fabrics. The expo was attended by 155 exhibitors from twenty states and Europe. Henry was one of the organizers. The exposition served as a platform from which the city could promote itself as a clothing manufacturing center. Cincinnati benefitted from local coal and water sources for power, access to Southern cotton, and rail and water transportation for distribution of products. [124]

The clothing industry may have played a role in Cincinnati's last major outbreak of smallpox. Widespread vaccination sharply reduced the frequency and severity of smallpox epidemics during the nineteenth century. Outbreaks were still sporadic and, in 1882, Cincinnati was in the midst of one. More than four thousand cases were reported and 1,249 deaths resulted.[125]

As the disease spread, panic set in and the public demanded greater action from the municipality's health department.[126] It was understood that smallpox is primarily contracted through close contact with infected individuals but that it could less often be passed along via vectors such as clothing. The clothing industry not only brought workers together in close confines but then sent clothes into the community. One afflicted worker could thus infect co-workers as well as the public. In order to allay fears and preserve business, Cincinnati's textile firms published an affidavit in May 1882. Signed by the coalition's president Henry Mack, the document outlined how the industry was proactively doing its part to stem the outbreak. The firms, for example, promised to only hire workers who could provide proof of recent immunization.[127]

Mack, Stadler & Co. would remain strong for another two decades. Harmon retired in 1868 and the next generation of Macks gradually entered the business—Harmon's son Isaac in 1865, Harmon's son Marc in 1870, Henry's son Harry soon afterwards, and then finally Harmon's son-in-law Henry Newburgh in 1879.[128]

Henry withdrew as the last of the first-generation partners in 1884 in order to give his full attention to his public and religious activities.[129, 130] The Mack children took over running the firm, although Henry and Harmon still owned the six-story warehouse. The elder brothers also likely remained in an advisory capacity.

The 1880s were a tumultuous period for corporate-labor relations. The labor movement was on the rise and wanted a share of the Gilded Age profits. The May Day strikes of 1886 were a watershed for organized labor. Unions across America began striking on May 1 in demand for an eight-hour workday and ten percent pay raise. The May Day strikes culminated in Chicago's tragic Haymarket Square riots and would eventually inspire creation of Labor Day. On May 11, Cincinnati's cloth cutters union struck, walking out of Mack, Stadler & Co. and the city's other clothing firms.[131]

Then, early in the morning of November 20, 1886, a fire broke out in the Mack, Stadler & Co. warehouse and quickly spread to an adjacent warehouse. Estimated loss in building and stock to the Mack firm was $335,000 with $228,500 covered by insurance. Fortunately, no deaths or serious injuries occurred.[132] The House that Mack Built would not survive long under the second generation's watch. The senior partner, Isaac H. Mack, died in the fall of 1894. Without his leadership, the remaining partners dissolved the company the following year. The merchandise of the one-time behemoth was auctioned off at a fraction of its value.[133-135]

Embroiled with the Grants

Though contemporary accounts described Henry as "honorable" and of "excellent character," it was through a shady business deal that he gained some notoriety and inadvertently impacted national politics.[136] The episode in question revolved around the father of General Ulysses S. Grant.

Although the Civil War, as mentioned, created a huge market for uniforms, it was a mixed blessing for the clothing industry because it threatened to cut off the raw material, cotton, that was required to meet that demand. Because the cotton trade helped finance the Confederate war effort, the federal government gradually prohibited commerce in Southern cotton. The effect of this restriction was to drive up cotton prices, from ten cents per pound in 1860 to sixty-eight cents per pound just two years later. Speculators managed to maintain some cotton flow to the North, albeit a trickle, through legal loopholes and the black market.[137]

In August 1862, Ulysses S. Grant became the commander of the Army of the Tennessee. The Department of the Tennessee encompassed portions of Tennessee, Kentucky, and Mississippi, and served as the major portal for the illicit cotton trade.[138]

In December 1862, Jesse Grant (the general's father) and the Mack brothers struck a deal. Jesse Grant signed a contract promising to use his influence with his son to obtain a special permit that would allow the Macks to trade with the Confederacy. The Macks, in return, promised to provide the money and to share one-fourth of their profits from the trade with Jesse.[139, 140]

That same month, Jesse wrote to and visited his son in an effort to fulfill his part of the bargain. Jesse was reportedly accompanied by the Macks. When Ulysses Grant refused to sign a permit, the Macks withdrew from the agreement. Jesse Grant responded by suing the brothers for breach of contract. The Cincinnati courts ruled in favor of the defendants.[141]

The case would have remained buried in some dust-covered docket had it not been for the infamous General Order No. 11. Though American Jews have enjoyed a great deal of freedom and tolerance, anti-Semitism often runs quietly under the surface. In trying times, Americans frequently turn their Jewish neighbors into scapegoats. An often-cited example of this phenomenon occurred in the wake of the Grant-Mack contract.

Many Northerners, including General Grant, considered trade with the Confederacy as tantamount to treason and believed the Jews were the principal conspirators in the illicit cotton trade. In truth, only a fraction of these traders were Jewish. Historians have concluded that the failed Grant-Mack deal was the final straw causing Grant to issue Order No. 11, which proclaimed that "Jews, as a class violating every regulation of trade established... are hereby expelled from the department within the twenty-four hours." A public uproar followed and a delegation of leading Jewish citizens traveled to Washington to meet with President Lincoln. Lincoln immediately revoked the order.[142] Historian Bruce Catton summarized the motives behind Order No. 11:

> Back of this order were two moving causes.... The obvious immediate one was cotton [speculation].... What had touched Grant off was the alliance made by his father [with the Macks]....But the invisible cause of the order—the thing that turned it from a simple tightening up of controls on illicit cotton brokerage into a blind, shotgun blast at the Jewish people—was the fact that Grant at all times reflected the age in which he lived.[143]

The incident would have again faded into obscurity had it not been for Grant's 1868 campaign for the presidency. Realizing how unlikely they were to defeat the Republican war hero, the Democrats revived the Grant-Mack fiasco. The Democratic press, including Cincinnati's own *Enquirer*, twisted the story so as to insinuate that Grant had used his influence to help his father speculate on the cotton market.[144, 145] The Democrats also tried to use Order No. 11 to make him appear an anti-Semite.[146]

Though the scandal failed to derail his candidacy, Grant later appointed several Jews to important federal posts. David Eckstein, for example, was appointed to be United States consul to Victoria, Vancouver Island shortly after Grant's election and in response to a written plea by thirty prominent

Cincinnatians. Amongst those thirty signatures was that of Henry Mack![147] These appointments may have been an attempt to quiet the accusations of anti-Semitism raised by the affair.[148]

Author's note: For additional information about the prelude to, event itself, and aftermath of Grant's General Order No. 11, please read Jonathan D. Sarna, <u>When General Grant Expelled the Jews</u> (New York: Schocken Books, 2012).

Cincinnati in 1841, the year of Henry's arrival. As viewed from the North, the Miami and Erie Canal is in the foreground while the Ohio River and Kentucky beyond are in the distance. [source: New York Public Library Digital Collection]

Henry and Rosalia Mack in the early 1860s. Henry was outfitting Union soldiers with uniforms and heading the Hamilton County Military Committee. [source: Michael W. Rich]

Henry was responsible for the fundraising for Bene Yeshurun's first place of worship. The synagogue opened on Lodge Street in 1848. [source: The Public Library of Cincinnati and Hamilton County]

The Talmud Yelodim Institute (1849-1866) was Henry's brainchild. TYI was housed in this building, erected in 1855 adjacent to the Lodge Street Synagogue.

Isaac Mayer Wise was the founding father of the American Jewish Reform Movement. His career, along with the course of Reform Judaism, took flight when he assumed the rabbinical post at Bene Yeshurun. Henry persuaded Wise to leave Albany for Cincinnati, where the two friends worked together to build the movement and made Bene Yeshurun its hub. [source: American Jewish Archives in Cincinnati, Ohio]

The cover to the music program for the 1866 dedication of Bene Yeshurun's new home. Henry supervised the fundraising and construction of the Plum Street Temple that is now a National Historic Landmark. The program's title, 'Progress March,' reflects the congregation's role in leading American Judaism into the modern world. [source: Sheridan Libraries and University Museum of Johns Hopkins University in Baltimore, Maryland]

The silver plaque presented to Henry in recognition of his chairmanship of the Plum Street Temple Building Committee. [source: Michael W. Rich]

Henry in 1872. He was now considered one of the Queen City's "leading men." [source: James Landy, *Cincinnati, Past and Present* (Cincinnati: M. Joblin & Co., 1872)]

Another public structure built under the guidance of Henry Mack. Pictured are the frontage and spacious reading room of the Cincinnati Public Library. Henry provided the dedication speech at its grand opening in 1876.

The magnificent Cincinnati Music Hall was completed in 1878. Henry was a key fundraiser for the Hall which has since been designated a National Historic Landmark. [source: *Harper's Weekly*, May 11, 1878]

BENJAMIN HARRISON,
674 North Delaware St.

Indianapolis, Ind., Nov. 16th. 1888.

Henry Mack, Esq.,
    Cincinnati, O.

My Dear Sir:-

    I beg you to excuse the delay in acknowledging your kind letter of congratulations of Nov. 9th. You will readily understand why it has been impossible for me to give prompt attention to the letters of my friends. I heard, during the campaign, of your work in our behalf and am very much obliged to you for that also. While very much pressed for time, I shall be glad, at any time you may desire to call, to see you at my home.

        Very truly yours,

        Benj Harrison

SC-14135. American Jewish Archives, Cincinnati, Ohio.

Benjamin Harrison's invitation for Henry to visit him at his Indiana home. Henry accepted the invitation, expecting the president-elect to offer him, as promised during the campaign, a cabinet-level position in the new administration. Henry would return to Cincinnati disappointed. [source: American Jewish Archives in Cincinnati, Ohio]

This *Cincinnati Post* cartoon depicted Henry in stereotypic German garb still seeking federal patronage after Harrison assumed office. (March 5, 1889) [source: NewsBank]

Henry in the 1870s. [source: American Jewish Archives in Cincinnati, Ohio]

Over the last two decades of his life, Henry proudly served on the board of trustees of the Cincinnati Southern Railway. [source: Z. Harrison, *Description of the Cincinnati Southern Railway from Cincinnati to Chattanooga* (Cincinnati: Spencer & Craig Printing Works, 1878)]

The Allemania Club's new home opened its doors in 1879. Henry chaired its building committee and delivered the official remarks at its opening gala. [source: *American Architect and Building News*, October 5, 1878]

Oil portrait of Henry Mack ca. 1890. Henry was at the zenith of his influence. Age and illness were, however, starting to take their physical toll. His once full face was beginning to look thinner. [source: Theodore Mack; photographed by Charles Kurtzman]

Henry and Rosalia Mack as they appeared at the time of their fiftieth wedding anniversary. The effect of prolonged illness is apparent in Henry's gaunt features. (*Kentucky Post*, September 11, 1896) [source: NewsBank]

Contributions to Reform Judaism

In his day, Henry Mack was recognized for his commercial success, but it was through his contributions to Judaism that his influence continues to be felt. He was an important pioneer and catalyst in American Reform Judaism.

Napoleonic Germany was the birthplace of Reform Judaism, and its ideas were brought to the United States by German-Jewish immigrants. Many Jews viewed Orthodox Judaism as cumbersome and feared that its unique garb, language, and style of worship might alienate them from their non-Jewish neighbors. The Reform Movement was the means through which they adapted their religion to their new homeland. Some Reform practices were initially instituted by a handful of American synagogues. Lasting and widespread reformation, however, required a leader with the foresight, energy, determination, motivational skills, and organizational skills needed to transform ideas into reality. Rabbi Isaac Mayer Wise was this man, and with Henry Mack's assistance, he led the reformation.[149]

The Demmelsdorf congregation was undergoing its Reform transformation during Moses Mack's time as *parnoss* (congregational head). In 1837, a choir was introduced into services. Four years later, German prayers were interspersed with the traditional Hebrew ones. The synagogue was also remodeled, moving the *bimah* (religious podium) from its Orthodox central position to the more Reform position in front of the Torah ark. German epitaphs were appearing on the headstones of the congregation's cemetery.[150] The arrival of the reform-minded Mack clan must have thus been influential on Bene Yeshurun during the 1840s.[151]

Cincinnati's first congregation, Bene Israel, was founded in 1824 by Jews from England. The influx of German Jews during the next decade resulted in an ethnic rift and eventually to the formation of the predominantly German congregation Bene Yeshurun in 1840.[152]

Henry joined the new congregation and immediately assumed a leadership role. With the exception of his friend Rabbi Wise, it was Henry Mack who did the most to transform Bene Yeshurun into the leading Reform congregation in the United States. He was a central figure in nearly every major undertaking of the congregation over the next half-century. By the time of his death, worship in Bene Yeshurun had taken on all the trappings of modern Reform Judaism. Services were shortened, held in the vernacular, and accompanied by organ and choir music. Male congregants worshipped with their heads uncovered and were no longer segregated from female congregants.[153] The same trends had spread throughout the country, for by 1880, the majority of American Jews belonged to Reform's fifty congregations and were of Central European origin.[154]

When Henry Mack joined Bene Yeshurun, its congregants worshipped in a rented room. As the congregation grew in numbers and wealth, it was decided to erect a synagogue building. In 1847, when the congregation ran out of funds for the construction, Henry was chosen to head a new building committee. Under his guidance, the necessary funds were raised to complete the structure, which opened its doors on Lodge Street in 1848.[155] In recognition of his service, the congregation presented him with a silver goblet.[156] Henry served as the grand marshall and the honor of opening the synagogue's front doors and ark were given to the four oldest members of the congregation. Moses Mack was one of those four honorees.[157]

That December, at a meeting of the congregation, Henry proposed the creation of a primary school where Jewish children might be taught both religious and secular subjects. His proposal was probably a response to the poor quality of the Cincinnati public schools. Henry wrote in the Jewish periodical *The Occident* that the purpose of establishing the institution was "to supersede the necessity of sending our children to common or sectarian schools, and likewise to combine their general education with religious instruction from their very infancy."[158] The Jewish community considered a good education to be the key to social and economic advancement.

Henry's idea was received enthusiastically, and one year later students were enrolled in the new Talmud Yelodim Institute (TYI). Originally scheduled for February, the start of classes was delayed until September by the cholera epidemic.[159] The three story building that housed the school was built in part with a $5,000 donation from Judah Touro.[160] Henry served on the school's first board of trustees and would later serve as its school board president.[161] The Institute was considered by many to be the city's finest primary school. According to Henry, it was "the first Jewish school chartered in this country."[162] It reflected the vision of American Judaism that Rabbi Isaac Mayer Wise and Henry Mack embraced. As Wise pointed out in *The American Israelite* periodical, the "Institute is not orthodox, the children sit there with their heads uncovered and learn nothing of religion except the Bible."[163] The school also reflected the personality of its community in that its regular curriculum included German language and culture.[164]

The school marked its first decade of existence with a banquet. Our protagonist led the evening's toasts. First he raised his glass to "The United States – the mother and nurse of liberty." Next he remembered "the deceased members" of the community, specifically naming his brother Abraham's children. Finally, he toasted "Education – The only inexhaustible mine of everlasting treasures." One of the event's guest speakers was Rutherford B. Hayes, then city solicitor, later this country's nineteenth president.[165]

The average enrollment exceeded 150 students. Tuition during the 1860s was twenty to twenty-eight dollars. TYI offered such curricula as English, Hebrew, Penmanship, Drawing, Sewing, and Embroidery in order to prepare its pupils for a productive adulthood. Many poor and orphaned students were enrolled at no charge or at half-tuition. The school's solvency also depended upon donations. In 1863, the school administrators held a charity ball to celebrate TYI's thirteenth anniversary. Henry Mack, the outgoing board president was included in the festivities, offering a toast and a $100 donation towards the tuitions of poor students. More than $2,000 was raised that evening.[166-168] In 1868, the school was closed as a parochial school, becoming a Sunday morning religious school. The premise for the transition was that Cincinnati's public school system had improved. The more likely factor was the desire to Americanize Jewish children by integrating them into the public schools.[169-173]

The congregation next turned its attention to finding a permanent rabbi. Since its formation, Bene Yeshurun had endured a rapid succession of rabbis. By 1852, most of the congregants had become interested in religious reforms. Henry became the voice of the reformation wing of Bene Yeshurun. In a letter to *The Occident* in July 1852, Henry attributed the congregation's reluctance to reform to the minority Old Guard "who used that influence to crush everything that might tend to promote true religion…among the rising generation." Henry took the lead in rallying his band of young German immigrants to speak up. Henry recognized that the most important step towards transformation was having a spiritual leader with the charisma, organizational skills, and will to make reformation happen. He complained that the congregation "had never had a minister who could gain sufficiently the confidence of the people in promotion of true religion."[174] The congregation's Reform leadership recognized such a person in a vocal rabbi in Albany, New York. During the fall of 1853, Henry and a few colleagues wooed Isaac M. Wise away from his pulpit in Albany.[175]

Wise quickly set the tone for his tenure. He called together a meeting of Cincinnati Jewry to discuss the creation of a Jewish university. Henry Mack chaired this meeting, at which the Zion Collegiate Association was founded and given the charge of raising the money to create a Jewish center of higher learning. A banquet celebrating the college's opening was attended by such dignitaries as the governor of Ohio, Salmon P. Chase, who would later become chief justice of the U.S. Supreme Court. Zion College opened in the fall of 1856, but, due to flagging enrollment, closed after only a few years. Though it lacked staying power, lessons learned from the college's demise were later applied by Wise and Mack to the creation of the successful Hebrew Union College.[176]

Religious reformation may have contributed to the financial and social success of the American Jew. If they progressed unchecked, however, reforms threatened to erode Jewish identity. For example, due to the financial pressures of running a business in a Gentile world (e.g., Sunday laws), most Jewish businessmen kept their factories and shops open on Saturdays. Henry was disturbed by this affront to his faith. Consequently, in 1850, he led a group of Cincinnati's prominent Jewish businessman into organizing the Resolution Regarding Sabbath Observance. Henry chaired this meeting, at which thirty-two Jewish wholesalers resolved to keep their stores and factories closed on Saturdays if an additional twenty-five wholesalers pledged to do the same. In other communities across America, attempts were made to preserve the Jewish Sabbath, but none, including Cincinnati's, had much impact. As a result, observance of the Sabbath in modern America belongs primarily to the Orthodox.[177]

Henry Mack's next task was to help Bene Yeshurun build a new house of worship, as it had outgrown the Lodge Street Synagogue. Working with his brother Simon, he was a central figure in the planning, financing, and construction of the new edifice. Henry was chosen as chairman of the building committee responsible for finding a new lot and then overseeing construction of the edifice.

Upon accepting the chairmanship, Henry set forth his philosophy to build "a place of worship more suitable than the one now occupied by the congregation, both as to situation as well as in conformity with the demands of the spirit of progress and reform." The structure would serve to "shed an increased luster upon our faith, our city and ourselves." It was apparent that Bene Yeshurun was self-confident and had big plans to visibly show off its growing importance through its new home. The building was to be called a temple rather than a synagogue, in keeping with the congregation's Reform style of worship.

A plot of land was purchased at the corner of Plum and Eighth Streets. Planning began in 1860, but construction was delayed by the Civil War. On May 12, 1865 a procession of 2,000 Cincinnatians, including the mayor and several councilmen, made its way from the old Lodge Street Synagogue to the future site of the Plum Street Temple. The ceremony culminated in the reading of the congregation's history by Henry and then his laying of the cornerstone. As the cost of building skyrocketed, a handful of congregants cosigned bank loans on behalf of Bene Yeshurun to avoid further delays. Henry was one of those who cosigned these notes.

On August 24, 1866, following the structure's completion, another procession occurred, this time highlighted by a dedication ceremony. During the dedication, Henry received the key to the new temple from his daughter Henrietta. Later, he was given a hat-rack adorned with an engraved silver plaque in recognition of his services.

The temple was an impressive addition to Cincinnati's skyline and remains standing today, listed on the National Registry of Historic Places. Two minarets accent its Byzantine design. It cost a quarter of a million dollars to build, an extraordinary sum in those days, and boasts a seating capacity of more than 2,000 people. The Plum Street Temple symbolized the influence and wealth of the congregation it housed.[178-184]

Most of the building's cost was covered by auctioning off the sanctuary's prime seats. A total of $200,000 was raised. Thirty-nine seats sold for at least one thousand dollars each. Henry bid the eighth highest, receiving his seat for $2,500.[185]

Perhaps the most important and holy duty of a new Jewish settlement was the early establishment of a place to bury the dead. The Chestnut Street Cemetery served that purpose for Cincinnati until 1849.

The cholera epidemic of 1849 wiped out nearly 6,000 of Cincinnati's approximately 100,000 citizens.[186] The Chestnut Street Cemetery filled so quickly that the Jewish community did not have time to prepare for a new burial ground. They were forced to procure a temporary burial ground near Brighton House Hotel.[187] The first internment in the new permanent grounds in East Walnut Hills occurred in 1850.[188] In 1854, the city's two major congregations, Bene Yeshurun and Bene Israel, chose the land as their common burial ground, renaming the Walnut Hills Cemetery as the United Jewish Cemetery.[189] In 1871, many of the remains, including Isaac Mack's, that had been buried at Brighton were reinterred in Walnut Hills.[190]

Henry Mack served on its first board of directors.[191] The layout of the cemetery resembled that of other American Reform cemeteries. In traditional European burial grounds, men and women were buried in separate sections and in the order of their death, irrespective of family ties. In America, Jews established family plots.[192] Henry Mack would eventually be interred in the cemetery that he helped establish, where he now lies alongside his wife, father, mother-in-law, and three of his children.

The cholera epidemic impacted the Israelite community in another tangible way. Impoverished Jews dying from cholera were admitted to charitable hospitals that had no kosher foods, provided no Jewish rights to Jewish patients, and performed death bed conversions and Christian burials. In response, the first Jewish hospital in America was established in Cincinnati in 1850.[193] The Mack brothers were important contributors to this institution during its infancy. Henry used his fundraising skills, Abraham donated a large sum in memory of his two children that were killed in the railroad accident, and Harmon served as a trustee and later president of the board of the hospital.[194-196]

Further reforms took place after the Plum Street Temple's erection. During the brief span between 1871 and 1875, the congregation's board of trustees shifted from requiring the wearing of yarmulkes during prayer to actually banning headcovering. Three older congregants voiced such strong opposition that they were granted exceptions, being "permitted to wear their hats as long as they lived."[197] One of those three men, Harmon Mack, was remembered as the last living congregant "who retained the practice to keep his head covered during services."[198] In 1877, the second day of observance for Rosh Hashanah was eliminated. Five years later, the requirement of observance of the Sabbath in order to maintain membership in the congregation was stricken from Bene Yeshurun's bylaws.[199]

Mack's dedication to Bene Yeshurun is obvious from the preceding description of tasks he undertook. During his nearly fifty years in its fold, he served at various times as trustee, secretary (1847-49), vice president (1854-56) and twice as the congregation's president (1856-58 and 1867).[200-202]

The Foreman

With Bene Yeshurun now established as perhaps the country's preeminent Reform congregation, Wise could now use his influence as its leader to transform the religious practices of all American Jews to reflect the practices of his congregation.

Since his arrival in Cincinnati, Rabbi Isaac M. Wise had wanted to establish a center of higher learning where Jewish men could be trained to become rabbis.[203] American congregations had heretofore relied on the immigration of rabbis from Europe to fill their pulpits.[204] To create an American Jewish seminary as well as to meet other goals (such as a common Reform liturgy), Wise and Henry Mack organized a meeting of thirty-four of the nation's Reform congregations.[205] According to Henry Mack, this gathering of congregations was "for the purpose of forming a 'Union of Congregations,' under whose auspices to establish a Jewish theological Faculty, and devise other measures for promoting the prosperity of our religion."[206]

This meeting, held in 1873, created the Union of American Hebrew Congregations (UAHC). The organization's first executive board was elected and consisted of twenty members, including Henry.[207] As a member of the UAHC's Committee on Sabbath Schools, he helped fashion the template upon which generations of Reform Sabbath school children were educated. The committee's first recommendations were that the schools must have Hebrew classes, Jewish history classes, singing of religious songs, and preparation towards Jewish confirmation.[208] Wise introduced the confirmation service to America in 1845. With the endorsement from the UAHC, it replaced the Bar Mitzvah in Reform congregations as the culmination of a young man's formal religious education. Bar Mitzvahs occur at age thirteen. The Reform Movement argued that students were more mature and capable of taking on roles as members of the Jewish community if their education was extended to age sixteen.[209]

Within its first year of existence, the fledgling UAHC had established the Hebrew Union College. The college's inaugural board of governors was elected and the board, in turn, chose Henry Mack as its president.[210, 211] Following his two-year term, he remained on the board an additional year as a member of its Committee on Buildings and Supplies.[212] The college, built in Cincinnati, opened its doors in 1875 and today continues to train the nation's Reform rabbis.[213]

By the 1870s, American Judaism was about to transform again. Deteriorating conditions in Eastern Europe were beginning to drive its Jews towards American shores. America's established Reform Jews dreaded the arrival of their impoverished and seemingly uncultured Orthodox brethren. The earlier wave of immigrants had expended tremendous effort to assimilate and earn the acceptance of their Christian neighbors. Eastern European Jews threatened to undo all their efforts because they looked different, behaved differently, and spoke unsophisticated Yiddish.[214]

If it could not stem the tide, the Old Guard would at least attempt to accelerate the Americanization of these greenhorns. Relief societies began to pop up in different communities. The UAHC hoped to coordinate these various relief efforts. In 1879, the group began promoting its plan to colonize what they expected to be a few thousand immigrants into agricultural colonies throughout the Midwest. The colonies would be out of site, self-sufficient and acculturate its members into American ways.[215]

Growing impatient with the slow pace of the UAHC, New York's wealthy Jews established the Hebrew Emigration Aid Society of the United States (HEAS) in 1881. Our Crowd recognized that they were at the front line and immigrants would arrive at their city soon.[216]

The reigns to the relief coordination were officially handed over by the UAHC on June 4, 1881. On that day, delegates from the various relief societies gathered in New York City and agreed that HEAS should serve as the umbrella society. The HEAS role was symbolized by the election of its delegate, Judge Isaacs, to the chairmanship of the new HEAS. Perhaps to gain the UAHC's acceptance of its now secondary role, the convention elected UAHC's delegate, Henry Mack, to the vice chairmanship.[217, 218]

The new HEAS hoped to raise capital to pursue the UAHC's original colonization plans. These plans were washed away by the assassination of "tolerant" Czar Alexander II. The trickle of refugees transformed into a flood. Hundreds of immigrants became thousands, and then tens of thousands. Over the next quarter century, there was an exodus of more than 1.5 million Jews from the Pale. HEAS's resources were overwhelmed and the organization was dissolved in 1883.[219]

The work of Wise and Mack were now woven into the fabric of American Judaism and endure to this day. If Wise was the architect, then Mack was the foreman in the construction of the American Reform Movement.

Local Politics

Once Henry Mack established his financial success as a clothier, he was able to dedicate time and energy to public service. At the time that he entered public life, it was uncommon for Jews to be found in politics.

Cincinnati was an important political and economic center throughout Henry's residence in the Queen City. From 1840 through 1900, it was one of the country's ten most populous cities.

By 1859, he was already active in the local political scene, having joined the nascent Republican Party. A group of Cincinnati's Republican leaders, Mack amongst them, invited presidential candidate Abraham Lincoln to speak in Cincinnati. Lincoln accepted, being welcomed to Cincinnati in September 1859 by a delegation of prominent Republican citizens. The delegation's roster included Henry Mack and future U.S. president Rutherford B. Hayes. The delegation introduced Lincoln to a crowd of three to four thousand supporters who were then to witness one of the most important campaign speeches in American history. Lincoln's two and one-half hour speech "contributed more to the Republican victory of 1860 than any single speech he ever made" by attacking Stephen Douglas's slavery stance so as to divide the votes of the Southern from the Northern Democrats.[220, 221]

Mack was elected in 1859 from Cincinnati's Second Ward to serve on the city council. He introduced the bill that provided for the city's first effective public transit system.[222, 223]

In Cincinnati's earlier years, daily travel for most citizens was restricted to walking. Consequently, one lived close to where one worked. Only the affluent could afford a horse and carriage.[224]

During the 1830s through 1850s, major cities adopted the first legitimate form of transportation – the horse-drawn omnibus. This vehicle could carry a dozen passengers but was limited in its usefulness by the poor roads of the era. Rough muddy streets slowed the animals and jostled the passengers.[225]

In 1832, New York City introduced the horsecar line, an urban version of the railroad. Horses now pulled their passengers along rail tracks that were embedded in the roads. The rails allowed for smoother, quicker travel. This form of mass transit spread to New Orleans in 1835, Boston in 1856, Philadelphia in 1858, and then Baltimore, St. Louis, and Cincinnati the following year.[226]

Mack and his fellow councilmen granted five routes to different groups of investors.[227] Rumors soon circulated that some councilmen had been "bought" by stockholders and merchants who desired to influence the route locations.

Henry voted in favor of creating a committee that would investigate the accusations. He and four of his fellow councilmen were chosen and eventually they declared the accusations to be false. Suspicions swirled around all of the city council members such that even Mack was called to testify on his own behalf. When Henry was "suddenly" obliged to leave town for urgent business on the very day he was scheduled to take the stand, one councilman voiced displeasure at the business trip's convenience. Instead, Henry offered a written testimony which was rumored to have been prepared by the attorney who also represented one of the winning bidders for routes. When asked by the press about his role in the choice of bidders or routes, Mack vehemently denied any improprieties.[228, 229]

It was only a couple months earlier that the newspapers had recognized him for turning away a bribe from a contractor seeking to provide the city's street cleaning service.[230]

As chairman of the council's Committee on Sewerage and Drainage, he was also instrumental in the development of Cincinnati's modern sewage system. By mid-century, it was realized that poor sanitation was a cause of epidemics. Three major cholera epidemics struck the United States during the first half of the nineteenth century. The 1849 epidemic took thousands of Cincinnati lives, including Henry and Rosalia's first child, Isaac.[231, 232] It may have been the memory of this tragedy that set him to the task of improving the Queen City's sanitation.[233]

In 1860, Cincinnati's mayor and civil engineer accompanied Henry on a visit to Philadelphia, Manhattan, and Brooklyn. The trio studied those municipalities' sewers and drainage. His tour convinced Henry of the necessity of an effective sewer system: "I am convinced that the question of City Sewerage is one of the most important which claims the attentive consideration of the municipal authorities of our large cities." He described to city council the structures and connections of each city's system as well as how the funding and maintenance of each occurred. He also noted apparent shortcomings such as individual neighborhoods building and maintaining separate sewers and the failure to consider the increasing demands imposed by population growth. While refraining from specific recommendations, Henry did endorse the concept of a city-wide sewage and drainage system that would be built and maintained publicly and "which may grow with our growth." He went on to suggest that the system should start immediately with construction of sewers on Vine and Walnut Streets, which just so happened to pass through his Second Ward, thus benefitting his constituents.[234, 235]

Reducing contagion would require more than just building a modern sewage system. Until the middle of the nineteenth century, urban sanitation was limited to residents burying trash in their yards or dumping it into the street. Animal feces, rotting food, and other refuse piled up in the streets. The less fortunate might pick through the waste looking for useful items to salvage or sell. Roaming bands of hogs devoured the food scraps.[235]

As cities grew in population, so did the garbage. Disease was attributed to the decaying trash and omnipresent swine. The populace increasingly complained about the clutter, stench, and scavenging animals.

In 1860, Cincinnati's government responded by becoming one of the first to mandate city-wide garbage collecting and street cleaning. City council banned pigs from streets and other public places. Residents were required to discard their trash into closed containers to be placed near the street. The city contracted garbage collectors to haul away the trash weekly. Except for the use of garbage trucks in place of carts, little has changed in the process over the past century-and-a-half. During council's deliberations, Henry endorsed the plan, remarking that he had directly observed their successful implementation in cities to the East when studying their sewage systems.[237-239]

That same year, Queen Victoria's eldest son went on a diplomatic tour of Canada and the United States. Upon learning that the Prince of Wales would be visiting North America, the city council voted to invite England's future King Edward VII to their city. The majority of councilmen voiced that a royal visit would boost the stature of Cincinnati and perhaps lead to commercial ties to Great Britain. Speaking for the minority, Mack objected to spending taxpayers' money on a monarch:

> [I] was born in a country governed by Kings [and] could not live under their rules....We [Americans] were opposed to the rule of Princes, and we would make fools of ourselves to spend money for their reception.

Towards the end of September, a gala was held at Pike's Opera House in the prince's honor. Henry Mack did not participate in the reception committee.[240, 241]

Henry would serve only one term on the city council. He was defeated for reelection. His loss was attributed to short-sighted voters who opposed the cost of his public works advocacy.[242]

In spite of his failed reelection attempt, the ex-councilman's political influence was on the rise. In February 1861, President-elect Lincoln's office in Springfield, Illinois was inundated with petitions for presidential appointments. One petitioner named Morris J. Marschuetz sought to be the customs service appraiser in San Francisco. He turned to Henry for a letter of recommendation. In his letter of support to Lincoln, he described himself as Marschuetz's "guardian" who had known the applicant "from his boyhood up." Marschuetz may have hailed from the Demmelsdorf region and been related to Henry's boyhood school teacher Jakob Marschuetz.[243, 244]

In 1861, Ohio Governor David Tod appointed Mack to the Hamilton County Military Committee. He chaired the committee through most of the Civil War.[245]

The principal and founding function of Ohio's county military committees was the oversight of the recruitment of soldiers.[246, 247] During the Civil War, it was the responsibility of counties to meet recruitment goals established by the federal government. The military committee of each of Ohio's eighty-eight counties would raise and distribute the bounties used to recruit soldiers from within its respective boundaries. When recruitment quotas were not reached, drafts were ordered by the governor to make up the deficit.[248]

As the war dragged on for years, these committees took on the unforeseen role of protector of soldiers' families. These families became increasingly destitute, having lost their loved ones' incomes. Military pay was generally much less than pre-war civilian income. Wives and children of incapacitated soldiers and war widows and orphans were particularly desperate. In nineteenth-century America, the federal government did not provide public welfare. Instead, local governments and private charities provided the bulk of the assistance. Within this context, the military committees helped raise and distribute aide to needy military families.[249-251] During the particularly dark days of November 1864, the committee organized a public meeting to discuss the impending winter of dismay. Henry Mack estimated that 4,000 families of soldiers in Hamilton County were already receiving public support. In response to the committee's call for help, charitable groups organized a series of benefits that raised approximately $50,000. The program, entitled Testimonial to Soldiers' Families, included personal appearances by such dignitaries as the lieutenant governor and Union generals Joseph Hooker, William Rosecrans, and August Willich.[252]

The Hamilton County Military Committee met every day during the war and committee members served without pay.[253, 254] In recognition of his tireless efforts as chairman of his county's committee, in 1864, Governor Brough awarded Henry Mack the honorary commission of colonel.[255]

After the war, President Andrew Johnson visited Cincinnati. The reception committee chosen to meet Lincoln's successor in the fall of 1866 included "Colonel" Mack.[256]

Mack's support of religious education has already been described in regard to his efforts on behalf of the Talmud Yelodim Institute, Zion College, and Hebrew Union College. His interest in public education translated into fourteen years on the Cincinnati Board of Education (1863–69, 1871–77, and 1887–89).[257]

The Cincinnati Public Library was under the auspices of the board of education. As such, the board appointed from its own ranks most of the members of the Library's board of managers. Henry was thus appointed to a one-year term on the board of managers in 1874.[258] The experience gained with the building of the Lodge Street Synagogue and the Plum Street Temple helped him to chair the building committee of Cincinnati's new Public Library, which opened in 1874.[259-261] The project cost $383,600 and the new edifice housed 71,000 books with room to accept another 180,000.[262] At the dedication ceremony on February 25, Henry presented a summary of the project. He concluded his speech by espousing his philosophy that education is one of the foundations upon which a modern and democratic society is built and how he hoped the new library would contribute to that cause:

> May increased supplies of wisdom, knowledge and virtue be its rich and abundant fruits for us and our posterity. May it be sanctified to the highest interests of the community that here at least knowledge may not be separated from the tree of life, and that constituting, as it will, the complement and the crown of our great republican system of popular education, may it do its part in bearing up and sustaining for generations to come a well-compacted and unperishable fabric of intelligence, freedom, philanthropy and patriotism.[263, 264]

Mack was a member in 1869 when the school board issued its famous ruling that discontinued the practice of reading the King James Bible in the Cincinnati schools. Curiously, the ruling was not intended as a wedge to separate church from state in the schools, but rather had the more practical impetus of being a compromise with the Catholic community in an attempt to merge the public system with the competing parochial system. The school board believed that Catholics would be unwilling to join a public school system in which the Protestant version of the Bible was read.[265] A group of Cincinnati citizens challenged the ruling, but the board's decision was upheld by the Ohio Supreme Court in 1873, in a case that gained much national attention.

The case has been hailed as the first major victory for those favoring strict separation of church and state. The controversy over Bible reading and its companion issue, prayer in the public schools, rages on today. Surprisingly, Henry Mack voted with the minority of the school board that favored Bible reading. His vote opposed that of the board's other Jewish member, Edgar Johnson, and the opinions of most of Cincinnati's Jews.[266] Henry argued that both the Old and New Testaments taught the kind of morality that was beneficial to children of all faiths. His comments found their way into newspapers across the nation.[267]

During his fourteen years on the board, he served on such standing committees as buildings and repairs, funds and taxes, discipline, and German department.[268] Nearly one-fourth of Cincinnati's residents were German and more than half of the Cincinnati students who attended the municipal schools were enrolled in its German department—classes taught in both English and German.[269]

Henry usually chaired each new board of education session. It was during these opening sessions that new officers were elected. The opening session of the 1872 board was called to order by a different chairman because this time Henry had been nominated for school board president. In spite of the board having a Republican majority, Henry lost in a twenty-five to twenty vote to a Democrat.[270]

In 1874, the Democrats unseated the Republicans as the majority party on the board.[271] The following year, Mack was forced to run as an Independent.[272] The new board replaced him as director of the Public Library, a decision that the Republican press denounced as due in part to him being a "Hebrew and is [thus] fair game for persecution by the Democrats" who now controlled the board. Two years later, he was off the board.[273]

During the 1870s, he served on the Cincinnati Board of Trade, including a two-year stint on its board of directors.[274] When the board of trade decided to spin off a board of transportation in 1876, Henry helped draft the new organization's constitution and bylaws and then served as its first vice president.[275, 276]

His public service extended to the building of Cincinnati's Music Hall. In 1875, Mack was elected to serve as one of the fifty founding stockholders, more formally known as the Board of Music Hall Incorporators. He helped solicit donations as a member of the foundation's Subscriptions Committee. The Hall was completed in 1878 at a cost of approximately $450,000 and was designated as a National Historic Landmark in 1975. It is home to the Cincinnati Symphony Orchestra and Cincinnati Pops Orchestra. Festivals and industrial exhibitions have filled its halls. The Music Hall hosted the 1880 Democratic National Convention.[277-280]

When Ohio Dried Out

In 1869, having already contributed to local politics, Henry Mack made his first foray into state politics by running for the Ohio Senate. He was defeated in this outing, smeared by the Democratic press's resurrection of the Mack-Grant cotton fiasco. In the weeks before the 1869 election, *The Cincinnati Daily Enquirer* chastised both President Grant and Mack. The newspaper reminded readers that Mack was running for state senator and that the attempted deal with Jesse Grant was "illegal" and "disgraceful."[281] In another article, it falsely suggested that Mack actually obtained the "illegitimate" contract, pocketed a $40,000 profit and then double-crossed Jesse by refusing to share those profits. The article then bombastically warned voters that "this is the kind of man that is proposed shall represent Hamilton County in the highest branch of the State Legislature, an office where the strictest integrity is required."[282] A third *Enquirer* editorial hammered home its point: "Honest and intelligent Republicans, we ask, what do you think of such transactions? Ought it not to be rebuked at the polls?"[283] The Republican counterpart, the *Cincinnati Commercial Tribune*, countered with its own editorial defending Mack as a "merchant of irreproachable character."[284]

In the wake of his defeat at the hands of the Democratic press, Mack struck back. He spearheaded the creation of a new German daily newspaper. The Cincinnati Courier Company was incorporated with the stated purpose of promoting the Republican Party's agenda.[285] The company published the daily *Wochen-blatt* and Sunday *Taglicher* from 1869 through 1874.[286]

A few years later, Mack's political ambitions were again thwarted by the reverberating cotton deal controversy. After Ulysses Grant's election to a second term, the president was contemplating whom to appoint as the next *Cincinnati postmaster*. Mack's candidacy was endorsed by several prominent Cincinnatians including Subtreasurer William Davis. Grant was overheard saying "I think I will put Mr. Mack in there." To Mack's dismay, influential advisors dissuaded Grant by reminding him of potential public perception should he nominate a participant in that old cotton scandal.[287, 288]

With the approach of the presidential election of 1876, Mack's political star was clearly ascending. His hometown would host the Republican National Convention. He was chosen to serve on the executive committee responsible for organizing the Convention to be held at Exposition Hall in mid-June.[289] Frederick Douglass was one of the featured speakers. Attendees watched as Mack's old acquaintance Rutherford B. Hayes overtook James Blaine on the seventh ballot to secure the nomination.[290]

Hayes then faced New York Governor Samuel Tilden in what was shaping up to be one of the most contentious elections in U.S. history. The predominantly Democratic South favored Tilden while the largely Republican North backed Hayes.

Mack spoke on behalf of Hayes a week before the election at a Republican gathering in the Queen City. The country was just emerging from the financial Panic of 1873 that occurred during Grant's watch. Mack tried to show how the U.S., in spite of having recently survived a bloody civil war and financial depression, was better off than European powers. America, under a Republican administration, was doing well.

> [T]he German masses are now financially prostrate. In England and Russia, France, Spain, and Italy, the same prostration of business exists. The United States is at present time more prosperous than any nation on the face of the earth.[291]

Unscrupulous tactics by both parties left the election without a victor. Neither man achieved the threshold number of electoral votes required and the deciding electoral votes resided in states that were contested due to counter accusations of fraud. Most egregious was the disenfranchisement of black voters by threats from the Ku Klux Klan and its ilk. A Constitutional crisis loomed. Renewed civil war even seemed possible.[292] Approximately fifty of Cincinnati's leading merchants petitioned Congress to find a peaceful solution for the sake of the country's business interests. The signees, including Mack, preferred election of either candidate over political limbo or a second election.[293, 294]

The Compromise of 1877 was struck to avert impending disaster. In exchange for Democratic acceptance of Hayes's win, the Republicans agreed to withdraw federal troops from the South, thus ending Reconstruction.[295]

The end of Reconstruction transformed the already bleak lives of ex-slaves into an unbearable existence. One immediate result was the Exoduster Migration of 1879. Approximately 27,000 black refugees fled Louisiana, Mississippi, and Texas hoping for better lives in Kansas.[296] Their new home state, however, did not have the finances to house, feed, and settle such a large group of impoverished people. Relief organizations sprang up in several communities. In Cincinnati, Mack and fourteen others organized fundraising efforts.[297]

By 1887, the specter of the cotton deal had faded and Ulysses Grant was no longer on the political scene. The Jewish press encouraged its readers to support Mack at the upcoming polls.[298] This time, a new generation of voters elected Mack to the Ohio Senate.

On December 29, the Hamilton County legislators, consisting of four senators and eight representatives, left for Columbus by train.[299] The following day, the delegation met in caucus to set an agenda for the upcoming months. As he did throughout his term, he served as the de facto leader of the caucus.[300]

The senate opened its sixty-eighth session on January 2. Mack was an active senator during his single two-year term. He introduced thirty bills, steering all but two to passage.[301, 302]

The 1888 session of the Ohio legislature was dominated by temperance legislation. The Temperance Movement was sweeping the nation. Ohio had already passed the Dow Law in 1886. The law's intent was to curb alcohol consumption by taxing each saloon $200 per year and allowing local governments to prohibit the sale of alcohol.[303]

Members of both political parties hoped to expand temperance legislation. It was primarily the Hamilton delegation that stood in their way. Its constituents were largely Germans, many of whom owned breweries, liquor stores, and saloons.[304]

The delegation managed to turn back the first bill that would have extended liquor sales prohibition to two miles beyond the boundaries of municipalities that outlawed such sales.[305] They could not, however, stem the tide further. The next bill, mandating public school instruction about the ill-effects of alcohol, became law.[306]

The two biggest battles lay ahead. Temperance politicians sought to increase the Dow tax and prohibit the sale of liquor throughout the state on Sundays. The latter proposal was known as the Owen Bill. In preparation for these battles, temperance and saloon lobbyists descended on Columbus.[307, 308]

In an attempt to avoid total defeat, the Hamilton senators struck a deal with their Republican colleagues. The four would support an increase of the Dow tax to $250 in exchange for a united front against the Owen Bill.[309-312] The tax increase passed but opposition to the Owen Bill eroded under withering pressure from the prohibitionist press. The Owen Bill passed the Ohio House and was now ready to be taken up by the senate.[313]

The bill's opponents had one remaining hope. The Owen Bill had been assigned to the senate's Committee on Municipal Corporations to vet before release to the entire senate. Henry Mack just happened to chair that committee. The crosshairs of Ohio's prohibitionists were now squarely focused on Mack.

Sensing its inevitable passage, the Hamilton caucus resorted to increasingly desperate tactics to weaken or stall the bill.[314] A motion to table the bill until the next year went down to defeat.[315] At the eleventh hour, Mack met with constituents and his fellow Hamilton senators to strategize.[316, 317] As chairman of the committee in charge of the bill, he refused to release it from the committee, thus preventing the senate from debating and then voting on it. One senator denounced the immorality of the Republican Party and another attacked Mack's behavior as "a usurpation of power that would not be tolerated."[318, 319] The temperance senators were able to strip the committee of the bill, allowing it to go directly to the floor for discussion. Mack countered that he had left the bill at his home in Cincinnati. He offered to return home to retrieve the manuscript, knowing that a mere week remained before the close of the current legislative session. The prohibitionists again outflanked him by having the house send another certified copy of the bill.[320]

The copy arrived the next day and debate commenced. Mack made his last attempt to weaken the bill. Risking anti-Semitic backlash, he moved to amend the bill to allow saloons to open after 1 p.m. on Sundays. He inferred that the bill infringed on his religious rights. Being a Jew, he argued, meant that he did not recognize Sunday as his Sabbath. He should not be compelled, therefore, by law to observe it as such. His motion lost twenty-one votes to eight. With the last obstacle eliminated, the Owen Bill was brought to a vote. It passed twenty-five votes to two, with the Hamilton delegation abstaining.[321]

The Owen Bill would stand for 116 years. His fight against this Sunday law received national and even international attention.[322] The newspapers overlooked that he had something personal at stake. His son-in-law owned Cincinnati's Labold & Newburgh – a liquor store.

The Promise

The height to which Henry's political star had ascended was on display in the presidential election of 1888. Incumbent Democratic President Grover Cleveland was pitted against the Republican challenger and former Civil War general Benjamin Harrison in what was shaping up to be a down-to-the-wire finish.

The path to the White House was a narrow one with the outcome pivoting upon three highly contested states – New York, Ohio, and Indiana. In the meantime, America's Jewish population was surging past 400,000 souls with large constituencies in the three aforementioned states.[323] This showdown would be the first time that the Jewish vote would help determine the outcome of a presidential race.

Harrison's campaign manager, Senator Matthew Quay, astutely recognized the importance of the Jewish bloc. He hoped to harness his candidate to this burgeoning electorate to help pull his candidate across the finish line.

But which Jew had enough name recognition and charisma to sway his brethren? Rabbi Edward Benjamin Morris Browne was recruited to find that person. His first choice was the influential and articulate Rabbi Isaac Wise. Wise, a staunch Democrat, could not support a Republican. Mack was the obvious alternative choice.[324]

Browne was dispatched to Europe to solicit Senator Mack's services. Quay authorized Browne to entice the Ohioan with the promise of a position in Harrison's cabinet should the Republican triumph. Traveling to Germany, Browne located "the aged legislator at a spa undergoing medical treatment." Mack agreed and, against medical advice, returned to America.[325]

He was scheduled to first speak at New York's Grand Opera House in support of Harrison's views on tariffs. "All went well until the morning of the speech when Mack awakened too ill to appear…. Browne had himself made up to look like Mack and delivered the speech himself." Upon recovering, Mack proceeded to give the speech in Albany and Indiana.[326-328]

Cleveland won the national popular vote but Harrison took the all-important Electoral College. Although Mack's influence on the Jewish vote cannot be accurately measured, what is known is that Harrison narrowly carried Ohio by fewer than 20,000 votes, New York by fewer than 15,000 votes, and Indiana by a razor-thin margin of 2,000 votes.

Rather than wait for the president-elect, Mack made the first move. Within days of the final tally, he wrote to the general offering his congratulations. Presumably he intended his letter to be a subtle reminder to Harrison of his obligation.[329]

Browne also penned a letter to Harrison. Not one to mince words, the rabbi bluntly recalled that Browne had agreed to join the campaign contingent "upon the condition that Judaism should be honored by the selection of a Hebrew to be a member of your cabinet. Senator Quay gave me his personal promise … that you would be willing to do so."[330]

A few strokes of his pen later, the letter took on a more conciliatory tone. He seemed resigned to the fact that Quay had likely overextended the number of promises to secure a victory and now Harrison was inundated with individuals seeking patronage. "In consideration of the circumstances surrounding you, I have concluded to release you of said promise if you so desire it."[331]

Unbeknownst to Browne, on the same day that Browne wrote his letter to Harrison, the latter sent a note to Mack inviting him to meet with him at Harrison's home in Indianapolis.[332] Henry arrived at the twenty-third president's homestead unaware that Browne had unfettered the president-elect from his campaign pledge.[333] Mack left empty-handed, thus denied his place in our nation's history books. In 1906, Oscar Straus would instead become the first Jew to fill a cabinet-level position.

Having been rebuffed for a cabinet-level position, eleven months later, Mack was in the nation's capital still lobbying for an appointment.[334] Local newspapers predicted he would become Cincinnati's next subtreasurer.[335] During the nineteenth century, the subtreasurer was an assistant to the United States treasurer and was responsible for the collection of federal revenues from a given region. Mack never received his appointment.

Author's note: For additional information about the role of Rabbi Browne in the election of 1888, please read Janice Rothschild Blumberg, <u>Prophet in a Time of Priests: Rabbi "Alphabet" Browne 1845-1929</u> (Baltimore, Maryland: Apprentice House Press, 2012).

The Chattanooga Choo Choo

In March 1876, the Cincinnati Superior Court appointed Mack to the Cincinnati Southern Railway (CSR) Board of Trustees. His tenure ended with his death two decades later. Also serving as trustee was Alphonso Taft, father of future president William Howard Taft.[336] Appointment to the five-member board was reserved for those "select men who, from their position in the community and from their known integrity, energy and capacity for business, may be safely confided in, and who will perform the obligation of their important office intelligently and uprightly, and for the benefit of the city and not for themselves."[337] Each trustee received an annual salary of two thousand dollars.[338]

The CSR was built at a time when railroad was King. Railroads were supplanting the canal system as the cheapest and most efficient means for transportation in our nation's expanses. If America's people, natural resources and products were its economic lifeblood, then the railroad was surely its arteries—the major means of transporting these components. At that time, the CSR was unique in that it was our country's only major rail system that was publicly owned and operated. In the wake of the Civil War, the economic opportunities of Southern reconstruction must have seemed irresistible to the Queen City. Cincinnati could tap into Southern natural resources, such as the cotton that fed its apparel industry, in exchange for selling Cincinnati's finished products in the formerly Confederate markets.[339]

The original board of trustees was appointed by the Superior Court in 1869. The local press supported a slate of potential candidates that included Mack.[340]

Construction of the railway began in earnest that same year but progress was slowed by political and financial challenges. Upon its completion in 1879, the CSR stretched 336 miles, including twenty-seven tunnels and 105 bridges. Two of these bridges were considered engineering marvels at the time. The Ohio River span was the longest truss bridge in the world while the Kentucky River span was America's first cantilever bridge. CSR terminated in the railroad hub of the South—Chattanooga.[341]

When Mack took his post, the railway was facing financial and administrative challenges that would divide the board into two opposing camps.

In 1869, the original $10 million bond was passed overwhelmingly by Cincinnatians 15,435 to 1,500.[342] America was in the midst of a railroad boom. Between 1866 and 1873, thirty-five thousand miles of tracks were laid in this country and Cincinnati had caught railroad fever.

The boom came to an abrupt end with the Panic of 1873. Just as a speculative growth in railroads fed the post-war economic bubble, the bubble was burst by a series of railroad failures. The depression forced eighty-nine of the nation's 364 railroad companies into bankruptcy and threatened to take down the CSR as well. Credit tightened, unemployment rose, businesses failed, and wages dropped.[343]

In the midst of this depression, December 1875, the CSR's chief engineer Thomas Lovett gave the board bad financial news. Lovett was the person responsible for overseeing the railway's construction. He projected that completion of the railway would require an additional $6 million infusion of capital.[344]

The board responded by asking voters to approve a second bond for the additional money. This request was met with some public and media resistance but passed in March 1876 by a 21,433 to 9,323 margin.[345]

Construction was also delayed by political hurdles and the Great Railroad Strike of 1877. The CSR had to gain the approval of the Kentucky and Tennessee legislatures in order to lay tracks across their states. U.S government approval was needed in order to span the Ohio River. The violent and widespread strikes of the summer of 1877 disrupted the entire industry.[346]

These mounting stressors caused the board to schism with its president Edward Ferguson on one side and Mack on the other. The split was rumored to be driven by petty jealousies over the differences in compensation between each trustee.[347]

The spat between Mack and Ferguson spilled into the newspapers. Henry believed that his annual compensation should be increased to $6,000. He justified his raise by noting that the railroad's financial difficulties pressed him into spending additional time providing business expertise. This time commitment forced him to give up his $6,000 per year salary from Mack, Stadler & Co.[348] Ferguson, a practicing attorney, also requested an increase in his CSR income for the legal advice he provided the CSR during this turmoil.[349, 350]

Both factions hinted at conflicts of interest. Ferguson's camp argued that Mack, Stadler & Co. sold goods to CSR contractors and asked the board to prohibit business relationships between contractors and firms controlled by board members. Mack's side countered that it was Ferguson who was influenced by these contractors because he also served as legal representative for some of the firms. The board was then asked to prohibit such relationships. The board did not act on either request. Recognizing their stalemate, Mack and Ferguson suggested the other resign, which neither did.[351]

Thomas Lovett became a victim of this boardroom tussle. Ferguson targeted the engineer as the scapegoat for the railroad's fiscal woes. The board president called for Lovett's dismissal, blaming him for the construction delays and cost overruns. The Mack faction sided with Lovett, arguing that Lovett had actually warned the board in advance of the expected higher costs but that Ferguson understated the cost to the public in order to get them to pass the bond. Ferguson's allies returned fire by attributing Mack's support to Lovett's hiring Emil Mack to be a clerk at the CSR station.[352] Unwilling to be the object of political wrangling, Lovett resigned in December.[353, 354]

It was soon apparent that the CSR would again run short of cash. With public opposition growing, Ferguson turned to the Ohio legislature for help. He convinced the legislature to pass the Ferguson Act. This act allowed the CSR to lease its existing rails to private firms in order to provide the steady stream of income needed to finish the project.[355-357]

These were dark days for the board. Their railway was in jeopardy and newspapers protested their perceived wasteful spending. Cries for their dismissal became louder when it was discovered that between 1875 and 1877, the trustees had received more than $40,000 in compensation. Mack's portion was $2,949.[358]

Mack publicly opposed passage of the Ferguson Act. He argued that allowing a handful of local companies to lease would invite graft and profit at the expense of the city's taxpayers.[359]

As the Ferguson-Mack feud played out in the newspapers, public support eroded. The trustees were painted as self-serving for asking for higher salaries while potentially harboring conflicts of interest. They were supposed to be stewarding the railroad through its financial difficulties. Mack's disclosure that the board had misled the public about predicted costs further undermined their faith in the board.[360]

Henry Mack's motives for opposing Ferguson and calling him out in the press can only be guessed. Was it moral outrage at Ferguson's duplicity? Was it an attempt to deflect the public's ire from himself? Did he have political aspirations? After all, the CSR board seemed to be a stepping stone to higher office. Alphonso Taft left the board in 1876 to serve as secretary of war in the Grant administration. Another trustee, Richard M. Bishop, successfully ran for Ohio governor in 1878 while serving on the board.[361] The most logical explanation would be residual bitterness from his personal financial loss in his suit against Charles Fries. The defendant's legal counsel had been none other than Edward Ferguson![362, 363]

Completion of the project was finally in sight. The trustees invited President Rutherford B. Hayes to accompany them as they toured on the nearly finished railroad. On September 12, 1879, the president, his attorney general, and General William Tecumseh Sherman took a passenger car roundtrip from Cincinnati to the Kentucky River Bridge and back again.[364]

The final rail was laid on December 10 and a few days later the trustees rode the first train to traverse the completed route. They were greeted by dignitaries and well-wishers upon their arrival at the Chattanooga depot. Henry Mack was made available to respond to questions from reporters.[365] On February 21, 1880, the first freight train completed the route.[366]

The much anticipated first passenger train arrived on March 5 to much fanfare. That train was immediately dubbed The Chattanooga Choo Choo, eventually entering the American lexicon as the title of The Glen Miller Band's 1941 hit song of the same name.[367, 368]

The railroad conglomerate Cincinnati, New Orleans & Texas Pacific Railroad (CNO&TP) became the new lessee in 1881, signing a twenty-five year contract.[369] This new holding company issued $3 million in stock, just over half of which was snatched up by a New York investor. The remaining stock was purchased by more than 100 Cincinnatians. Henry invested $25,000 of his own money. Harmon and three of Harmon's and Henry's sons bought another $65,000. The Macks now owned three percent of the new railroad.[370-372] Nicknamed the "Queen and Crescent Route," there was now a direct route between Cincinnati and New Orleans. Over the next few years, tensions would arise between the CSR board and CNO&TP over the building of a railroad terminal in Cincinnati. When the cost of building the terminal exceeded the allocated funds, the CSR board attempted to make up the difference by raising the CNO&TP's lease payments.[373]

In 1888 and 1889, Henry Mack, who was now serving his term as state senator, introduced and guided to passage what became known as the Mack Bill. In preparation, he consulted with ex-Governor Richard M. Bishop, the former trustee of the CSR. The night before Mack introduced it in the legislature, the two men ironed out the details.[374] The Mack Bill allowed the CSR board to renegotiate the terms of the lease.

Senator Mack guided the bill to passage in his own branch of the legislature in March 1888 but the bill faced much opposition as it progressed to the Ohio House.[375] Mack now tried to influence his representative colleagues by hosting them and their wives on a lavish excursion to New Orleans on the Queen and Crescent. The couples dined on fine food, slept in luxurious quarters, and played cards late into the night. In return, the guests presented Mack with a gold headed cane and Mrs. Mack with a silver toilet set.[376, 377] The Cincinnati Southern Railroad apparently paid for the trip as well as hotel accommodations in New Orleans. When the press caught wind of this event, critics objected to what they decried as brazen lobbying. In one biting editorial, a columnist wrote: "The railroad has a little favor to ask, but it does not expect, of course, that its attention to the legislators will have the slightest influence on the latter in the matter of granting that favor. All the Cincinnati Southern company wants is that its lease be extended fifteen years."[378] The local Union Labor Party went so far as to suggest that the CSR trustees had premeditatedly worked to get Mack elected so that "Senator Trustee Mack" could get the extension through the legislature.[379] The next year, Mack hosted a second less extravagant round trip to Chattanooga. So many representatives accepted this invitation that the Ohio House had to take a recess because too few remained in Columbus to gather a quorum.[380]

Meanwhile, the Cincinnati Chamber of Commerce voted 390 to 312 against endorsing the bill.[381]

After the dust settled and the railroad was granted permission to renegotiate, CNO&TP refused to return to the table, stating that it was CSR's responsibility to provide the railroad terminal. The conglomerate hired Grover Cleveland as their legal representative. Cleveland was at the time between presidential terms. After years of courtroom wrangling, the two sides struck a compromise, resulting in a new long-term lease in 1901.[382-385]

Mack's role in the passage of his namesake bill would be perceived today as a conflict of interest. But through the Gilded Age glasses, it would have appeared as "business as usual."

It was during Henry Mack's time on the CSR board that the width of the country's railroad tracks was made uniform. Prior to 1885, the width of Southern tracks differed from that of Northern tracks. In 1885, it was decided that Southern railways, such as the CSR, would convert to Northern gauge. That change to all Southern railways was made in a mere thirteen hours on May 30, 1886![386]

Private Life

Henry Mack was well regarded for his generosity to others. More than once did he gave substantial sums of money to help his son-in-law Abram Newburgh salvage his foundering cigar factory.[387] I. J. Benjamin was a Jewish traveler whose diary was filled with descriptions of Jewish communities across Europe and America. Two entries in the diary note that financial assistance from Henry Mack made Benjamin's prolonged stay in Cincinnati possible.[388]

Rabbi Wise's son Julius spent much of his childhood in the presence of his father's good friend. He later reminisced about how he grew up admiring Henry. He wrote that "there never had been a time when I did not know Mr. and Mrs. Mack, and like everybody else who had known them it was to love and respect....Mr. Mack towered some ten feet above the ordinary run of men."[389]

A major hurdle overcome by Mack on his road to success was prejudice. Anti-Semitism and xenophobia were undercurrents throughout American history. General Order No. 11 was one of the more blatant examples.

The Dun & Co. credit reports exemplify how American Jews were singled out, distinguished from their Gentile neighbors. In various entries, the Mack brothers were identified specifically as Jews though religion should have had no bearing on their credit rating.[390] Entries on other Jewish merchants were often interspersed with stereotypic characterizations, such as shiftiness and cheapness.[391]

In 1877, another infamous act of anti-Semitism caught the nation's attention. Judge Henry Hilton refused entry of Jews to his Grand Union Hotel in Saratoga, New York. In response, forty-six of Cincinnati's Jewish firms, including Mack, Stadler & Co. took a stand against the hotel owner. The firms signed a letter of protest that promised to boycott A.T. Stewart & Co., Hilton's business.[392]

Sunday laws, alluded to earlier, were an important example of government sponsored anti-Semitism. These laws, usually enacted by state or local legislatures, forbade drinking, gambling, and business transactions from occurring on the Christian Sabbath. Sunday laws placed Jews at an economic disadvantage because they were already expected to refrain from working on their own Sabbath. Jews found guilty of violating Sunday laws were fined.[393, 394] Legal challenges to these laws often failed.[395, 396] The Queen City's social progressiveness was reflected in the fact that its Sunday laws were overturned in 1847.[397]

German-Jewish immigrants owed much of their success to their ability to adapt their ways to their new homeland. Nowhere was this more apparent than in the Reform Movement, but other facets of their lives were also adapted. The focal points for male socializing in nineteenth-century America were the fraternal orders, such as the Masons. German Jews in many cities found themselves unwelcome in Gentile social clubs. East Coast Jews were more likely than their Midwest brethren to face exclusion. As early as 1845, Henry belonged to a Masonic lodge in Cincinnati that boasted a blended Christian and Jewish membership.[398] Founded in the 1840s, B'nai B'rith lodges were the German Jews' response to exclusion from Gentile lodges. B'nai B'rith lodges sprang up in every major Jewish community and imitated Masonry with its secret handshakes, passwords, insignia, and ceremonies.[399]

The Cincinnati chapter of B'nai B'rith was founded in 1849.[400] Mack played an active role in B'nai B'rith, serving as a trustee for its local Mount Carmel Lodge and as president of the District No. 2 Grand Lodge (1884-1885).[401-403] District No. 2 included all of Ohio, Indiana, Kentucky, Missouri, Colorado, Kansas, and New Mexico.[404] He was also active in nondenominational fraternal orders, namely the Lafayette Lodge (Masonic), Cincinnati Lodge (Masonic), and Gibulum Grand Lodge (Good Fellows).[405, 406]

Cincinnati's German Jewish community also formed family social clubs. The Allemania and Phoenix Clubs provided venues for card games, receptions, banquets, dances, and thespian activities for all members of the family. They were precursors of country clubs.

Henry and his family were quite active in the Allemania Club, the social hub for Cincinnati's wealthiest and most influential German Jews. Henry was a founding member in 1849.[407] By the 1870s, it boasted well over 200 members. Henry served as its president in 1876.[408] By 1878, the society had outgrown its facilities. Henry chaired the building committee that oversaw construction of a new three story stone edifice at the corner of Fourth Street and Central Avenue. On May 1, 1879, Henry provided the opening remarks at the opening gala. He then presented the keys to the new facility to the Allemania's president.[409]

The gala was attended by 500 guests, including Governor Bishop. It was catered by the Allemania's food manager Gustave Lindeman. The dinner menu was notable for its first course—oysters. Oysters were a staple of affluent Gentile American gatherings. Shellfish, however, was forbidden by Jewish dietary law. Reform Judaism had disregarded many Jewish traditions but at least in public maintained *kashrut*. By the 1870s, many Reform Jews no longer observed kosher restrictions in the privacy of their homes but the Allemania festivities were public. Four years later, the same caterer served seafood again at the infamous "Trefa Banquet." This occasion celebrated the graduation of Hebrew Union College's first class of rabbis. The reaction from Reform Judaism's more traditional wing was to splinter off to form the Conservative branch of American Judaism.[410, 411]

Henry Mack resided in or near downtown Cincinnati for most of his adult life. As his family and wealth grew, he moved successively, presumably to larger houses. Until the 1870s, nearly all of Cincinnati's population crowded into the city's basin, bordered on the south by the Ohio River and to the north by its suburban heights. In 1858, one hundred sixty thousand inhabitants were concentrated into a mere five square miles. Walking served as the principal means of transportation, such that Cincinnatians were obliged to live within a few blocks to a mile of work.[412] Henry's stores and homes were in proximity to each other.[413] For the same reason, the Plum Street Temple was built in the vicinity of the Jewish community.

As noted previously, horsecar rail lines were introduced in 1859, providing some improvement in downtown transportation. The overlooking suburbs, however, remained essentially inaccessible, particularly during inclement weather. Horses struggled with their heavy passenger cars to climb the steep slopes that led out of the basin.[414]

The creation of four railway inclines between 1872 and 1876 made it possible for wealthier Cincinnatians to move to the suburbs above the downtown. The commute was improved further by the addition of a cable car line opened in 1885 between downtown and Walnut Hills. Consequently, such suburbs as Walnut Hills and Avondale to the northeast grew rapidly during the 1880s and became the suburbs of choice for affluent Jews.[415, 416] Henry and Rosalia moved with daughter Henrietta's family to Moorman Avenue in Walnut Hills in 1886.[417]

By the turn of the century, horsecars and cable cars had been replaced by electric streetcars. These street cars were rapid and cheap, making it possible for the less affluent to flock to Walton Hills.[418] Consequently, by 1900, nearly all of the city's well-to-do Jews moved further north to Avondale.[419]

The Mack children fondly recalled Henry and Rosalia's summer home in Mt. Airy. Mt. Airy was a village situated on the heights ten miles to the northwest of the downtown. Wealthy Cincinnatians spent their summers in Mt. Airy in order to escape the stagnant summer pollution that settled into the downtown river basin. The Macks already lived in Mt. Airy in 1870 when it was a blend of wealthy summer homes interspersed with farmland.[420] Their sixteen-and-a-half acre property stretched along the western side of Colerain Pike at its intersection with Shepherd Road and adjoined a hundred-acre fruit farm.[421] The Mack homestead was a working farm.[422-427]

Colerain Pike was managed by the Colerain, Oxford and Brookville Turnpike Company. In exchanged for tolls paid at intervals along the road, the company maintained the route. Until the advent of asphalt in the nineteenth century, Colerain Pike was paved via macadamizing. This process created a flat, durable surface through the layering of various sized gravel that was compacted to resist wear.[428]

The Pike served as the principal thoroughfare for bringing livestock from farms north of Mt. Airy to the processing plants in Cincinnati. During the nineteenth century, the Queen City was also known by its appellation "Porkopolis" because it boasted being America's largest supplier of pork. As each winter approached, farmers herded thousands of head of hogs, cattle, and even turkeys down the Colerain Pike on foot. Chicago would eventually overtake Cincinnati as the nation's meat processing capital, and trucks and trains would replace herding. But while the Macks lived in Mt. Airy, they would have watched the annual procession of ill-fated animals being driven to their demise in the dozens of Cincinnati slaughterhouses. Although all these plants have long since been shuttered, their legacy remains thanks to their animal byproducts. For example, tallow was used in the manufacture of candles and soap, giving rise to Jergens and the Fortune 500 powerhouse Proctor & Gamble.[429]

The couple frequently entertained family and guests on their estate over the years.[430] Daughter Louisa married Charles Newburgh on the grounds in September 1886.[431] Son Harry and his family stayed with his parents throughout the summer of 1889 during an extended visit from Kansas City.[432] Henry was an active participant in the suburban community. He served on its city council.[433] Just as he had done for Cincinnati, he hoped to modernize his second home town.

Although Mt. Airy offered fresh air and idyllic scenery, one-way travel to and from the city was still a three-hour trek.[434] There were no railways or well-paved roads connecting Cincinnati to its wealthy suburb. Even with macadamization, Colerain Pike could still be treacherous. Henry and some of his affluent neighbors hoped to change that situation.

The 1870s and early 1880s were the heyday for narrow-gauge railways in the United States. With their narrow tracks and lighter trains, these railways were touted as cheaper to build and better able to climb steep inclines than standard gauge versions.[435] These railways thus seemed ideal for rapid transit from the city uphill to suburbs that had limited funds for building.[436]

A number of the Queen City's suburbs scrambled to finance such railways.[437] In March 1876, the College Hill line opened, likely inspiring neighboring Mt. Airy to build its own.[438] Not only would travel to and from work become much faster but that accessibility promised to boost real estate values for properties along the route.[439]

In July 1876, the residents of Mt. Airy convened to discuss the financing and building of a seventeen-mile narrow-gauge railroad that would run from Cincinnati, through Mt. Airy out to the town of Venice in Butler County and terminate just over the state border in Liberty, Indiana. Mt. Airy residents predicted such a project would increase the value of their land from $100 to as much as $1,500 per acre. The track would run along Henry Mack's property on Colerain Pike.[440]

Henry agreed to co-sponsor the project. He and nine others incorporated the Mt. Airy, Venice, and Liberty Railroad.[441, 442]

Over the next several months, the course was surveyed, cost estimates prepared, and funding pledged. Enthusiasm must have waned as mention of the plan disappeared from newspapers for the next two years.[443] When a second attempt to raise $50,000 in bonds for the road failed in 1879, the project collapsed.[444]

Most of the Mack children moved out in order to either attend college or marry. Millie and Henrietta, however, along with their spouses and children, remained with their parents for years after marriage. Abram and Henrietta Newburgh, and later their three children, lived with Henry and Rosalia from the time of their marriage in 1872 until Henry's death. Two live-in servants tended to the needs of the family.[445, 446]

Further evidence of the family's wealth was their ability to vacation for extended periods of time. In 1884, for example, Henry and Rosalia spent two months vacationing in Florida.[447, 448] In 1890, the couple spent six weeks visiting their daughter Millie and her family in Dallas, Texas.[449, 450] Long-distance travel would have been by rail.[451]

In 1892, long before Forbes published its annual list of the world's 400 wealthiest individuals, the *New York Tribune* listed America's millionaires. Entered amongst the 4,047 millionaires was Henry Mack of Mack, Stadler & Co.[452] Adjusted for inflation, one million dollars in 1892 would be equivalent to more than $25 million today.[453]

Henry's extended family clustered around him as well. His father Moses and brothers Harmon and Abraham remained in Cincinnati from their times of immigration until their deaths. David along with three of Rosalia's siblings and one of her cousins lived in the Mack home in 1850.[454] The last Mack family gathering may have occurred in November 1862 for Moses's eightieth birthday celebration. The patriarch was surrounded by five of his six living children, his twenty-seven grandchildren and many friends. The sons gave their father several presents, highlighted by a gold-headed cane to honor the occasion.[455] Moses died in February 1864.[456] As noted earlier, Simon moved to New York City in 1866. Julius lived in Cincinnati during the 1850s, in Memphis, Tennessee during the 1860s, in the township of Miami just to the east of Cincinnati during the 1870s, then lived out the remainder of his life in Toledo, Ohio.[457] David eventually returned to Bavaria with his wife and children.[458, 459] Henry's paternal aunt Babette arrived in the U.S. with her second husband Feiss Bamberger and their children in 1845 and settled in Louisville, Kentucky.[460, 461] Of the children from her previous marriage to Loeb Constine, one lived in Louisville, another child settled in Wilkes-Barre, Pennsylvania, while a third followed the Gold Rush to California.[462, 463]

Although they proudly identified themselves culturally as German, Cincinnati's German Jews lived separately from their Gentile counterparts. The two groups did share a common language and often interacted socially at festivals and in clubs. But in regards to family, business, and neighborhoods, they lived apart.[464]

German Jews usually married other German Jews as happened with Henry and Rosalia, their siblings, and their children. Interfaith marriage seldom involved the Queen City's nineteenth century Jews.[465]

They also rarely partnered in business with Gentiles. Negative stereotypes about Jews tended to keep Gentile banks from extending them credit. Christians often distrusted these "shrewd" or "shifty" merchants. Hence, the Macks merged with the Stadlers and Glasers.[466]

The ethnic enclave called the Over-the-Rhine community was home to the city's German Catholics and was located just north of the Miami and Erie Canal. German Jews concentrated in the district south of the canal.[467] During the mid-century, Henry lived within and served as councilman for the Second Ward that lay in this district.[468, 469]

In the Mack household, conversations with the children were in English. Because their children only understood rudimentary German, Henry and Rosalia reserved their native tongue for private conversations. Whereas Rosalia spoke English well, she was somewhat of a Germanophile, preferring to speak in German and dismissing non-German Jews as *Englische polten.*"[470]

During the 1840s and 1850s, the Bene Yeshurun day school boasted of its German curriculum.[471] When the congregation's rabbi retired in 1849, Henry presented him with a silver goblet that had been inscribed in English but honored him with a speech given in German. Well-wishers showered him with toasts and speeches, some in English and others in German.[472]

Contemporary newspapers also reflected this dichotomy. Rabbi Wise published two influential Jewish periodicals—the English language *American Israelite* and its German language sister publication *Die Deborah*.[473]

Until the Hebrew Union College graduated its first American rabbis, pulpits were occupied by rabbis imported from Germany. It is thus no surprise that their sermons were usually delivered in German.[474]

Assimilation was, of course, inevitable. The first generation of German Jews grew more proficient with their second language and more comfortable with American ways. The children had little impetus to perpetuate their parents' heritage and desired to fit in amongst fellow Americans.

As in all families, Henry's children could be a source of consternation. When, for example, his son Theodore publicly "defected" from the Republican Party in 1885, Henry must have felt some political embarrassment.[475, 476]

But it was another son, Emil, who caused his parents true consternation. Two of Emil's brothers became successful attorneys. His other siblings became or married successful businessmen. Emil, in contrast, was the black sheep of the brood. He was overly dependent upon his parents' goodwill. On his twenty-fourth birthday, his father presented him with a check for $500.[477] Meanwhile, he lived at home, working as a clerk for his father's Cincinnati Southern Railroad. During that time, at least one customer posted a complaint about Emil's behavior.[478] At age 30, he was a draughtsman at the Cincinnati water works.[479] Thereafter, his name is absent from the Cincinnati business directories, inferring his lack of steady employment. By 1894, he had several run-ins with the law, including at least three for passing bad checks. In all cases, his father paid off his debts. Emil had also seen his engagement to a jeweler's sister fail.[480-483] Henry's lack of confidence in his son was reflected in the elder Mack's will. All of his children were to receive equal shares of the estate. All but Emil were to receive the funds directly while Emil's portion was placed into a trust overseen by two of his brothers.[484] His death was equally unflattering. His body was found alone in a Chicago hotel room at the age of forty. The cause of his death was given as kidney failure but it was discovered that the gas line in the room was partially open.[485]

Henry traveled to Germany in 1888, seeking medical care at a spa, and visited his birthplace and mother's grave.[486] By now, Henry's features had taken on the appearance of the distinguished elder statesman. His passport describes him as standing five feet nine inches tall, bald with a white rim of hair, wearing a short gray beard with shaved upper lip, and darkly complected.[487] He was taller than average for the nineteenth century. One local was so struck by the senator and two of his friends as they strolled along a thoroughfare that years later he opined that "three handsomer or more aristocratic looking gentlemen never walked on even a European promenade."[488] This description is corroborated by a contemporary oil portrait.[489]

His health declined during the final years of his life, as exemplified by his aforementioned 1888 stay at a German spa and his late-life oil portrait that reveals his noticeably thinner face. In 1893, he suffered a stroke.[490] He disappeared from the public eye as evident by his name's absence from the newspapers. He was apparently too ill to return to his summer home in 1896; instead, the Mt. Airy property was leased to the Home for Incurables.[491] By June, he was experiencing "heart trouble" causing him to be "confined to his home" in Walnut Hills.[492]

The family's last celebratory gathering occurred on September 15, 1896 on the occasion of Henry and Rosalia's Golden Anniversary. All seven Mack children, along with the couple's friends, attended the party at the Mack home in Walnut Hills.[493] The out-of-town family must have realized that this would be the last time they would see their father alive and thus made the special effort of travelling all the way in from Texas and Missouri. In his account of the event, one grandson admitted that "Mr. Mack is not in the best of health."[494] The gauntness of his features were fully apparent in a newspaper sketch of the couple.[495]

Another grandson described Henry's health as only "fair" in November 1896.[496] His health rallied briefly only to succumb to colonic obstruction "after a long illness," on his seventy-sixth birthday.[497-499]

As his final birthday approached, it is said that Henry was already expecting death to take him on that day. He told his family that during his sea voyage to Germany in 1845, a clairvoyant Englishmen prophesied that Henry "would rise in business, should hold places of honor and trust, and that he would live to a ripe old age and die on his birthday."[500] His funeral was attended by many prominent Cincinnatians. Isaac Mayer Wise conducted the service and then delivered the eulogy. The great rabbi struggled to maintain his composure as he reflected on the life of "his dearest and closest friend."[501, 502]

Henry Mack quickly fell into obscurity following his death. Because he never held a federal office nor found heroism in war, the newspapers had little reason to celebrate his life. His obituary in *The Cincinnati Post* was a mere eight sentences long.[503] Without a memorial, building, or foundation bearing his name, there were no tangible reminders of his existence for future generations. His once renowned clothing firm was shuttered before his death and could thus no longer remind the public of its founder.

The value of Henry's public service was recognized in a relatively small way in 1976. Eighty years after his death, the Public Library of Cincinnati and Hamilton County honored him in an exhibit of twelve Germans who made important civic contributions to Cincinnati.[504]

The Mack Family in America

Though Henry and his brother Abraham were the first of the Mack clan to immigrate to America, it was not long before others in Henry's and Rosalia's families followed, perhaps on the advice of Henry and Abraham. The success of several of these individuals and their descendants elevated the family name to a prominent position in American Jewish history.

Herman and Lewis Mack settled in Milwaukee during the 1840s and quickly established a successful dry-goods business. During the 1860s, Lewis served as president of the Milwaukee Board of Aldermen and as chairman of the county board of supervisors.[505]

Julian Mack became a celebrated Zionist leader, U.S. appellate court judge, and personal advisor to President Franklin Delano Roosevelt. He served as the first Jewish overseer in Harvard University history and was instrumental in preventing passage of the school's infamous Jew quota during the 1920s.[506]

Henry's son Alfred, later a judge of the Hamilton County Court of Common Pleas, graduated from Harvard Law School in 1883, becoming one of the first Jews to do so.[507]

Julian and Alfred Mack were typical of the children of Cincinnati's German-Jewish settlers. Whereas the fathers succeeded through commerce, the sons often entered the professions.[508]

Walter Staunton Mack would head the soft drink giant Pepsicola during the 1950s.[509]

After graduating top of his class at Harvard Law School, Joseph Rauh, Jr. served as personal secretary to two U.S. Supreme Court justices. Known as a liberal flame, he chaired the District of Columbia's Democratic Party, co-founded with Eleanor Roosevelt and Hubert Humphrey the political watchdog organization Americans for Democratic Action, defended several prominent individuals in front of McCarthy's "communist witch trials," and served as an outspoken advocate of black civil rights. He was a central figure in the passage of the Civil Rights Act of 1964. In recognition of his many extraordinary contributions to American society, President Clinton posthumously awarded him the Presidential Medal of Freedom, the highest civilian honor.[510]

Emily Rauh was curator of the St. Louis Museum of Art and later a member of the Committee for the National Endowment of the Arts. Her marriage to newspaper mogul Joseph Pulitzer, Jr. led to their creation of one of the great private art collections in the world. In 2008, she donated $45 million and many important works of art to Harvard where she also served as an overseer. President Barack Obama awarded her the National Medal of Arts at a 2011 White House ceremony.[511, 512]

Edward Hirsch Levi married into the family. He served as president of the University of Chicago Law School, then as United States attorney general under President Gerald Ford, and later as president of the American Academy of Arts and Sciences.[513]

Robert Lehman was recognized equally for his financial savvy and his love of art. As president of the iconic Wall Street investment firm Lehman Brothers, he catalyzed a number of blockbuster mergers, acquisitions, and other capital activities. The collapse of Lehman Brothers in 2008, precipitated the Great Recession. He served as chairman of the board of the New York City Metropolitan Museum of Art. The bulk of his extraordinary private art collection, worth approximately $75 million at the time of his death, was willed to "The Met." It featured master works from the Renaissance and necessitated the building of the Lehman Wing to display the collection.[514, 515]

Described as "one of the great minds of the twentieth century," Lewis Charles Mumford was a social commentator, writer, and expert on architecture. His accolades included being the recipient of the Presidential Medal of Freedom, National Medal for Literature, National Medal of Arts, and National Book Award.[516]

Several of the Macks ventured into the frontier where they helped found fledgling Jewish communities and institutions. Herman and Lewis Mack were among the first dozen Jews to reside in Milwaukee during the 1840s.[517] Henry's brothers Simon and Martin were among the first dozen Jewish settlers in Columbus during the 1840s and Simon was one of the founding members of Columbus's first Jewish congregation—Bene Yeshurun—in

1849.[518, 519] In the early1840s, Henry's cousin John Constine settled in Wilkes-Barre, Pennsylvania, becoming one of the region's first Jews.[520, 521] John helped found the city's first Jewish congregation.[522] His family proudly recorded that John served as a conductor on the Underground Railroad and that his son Lewis was killed fighting for the Union during the Civil War.[523]

Henry Mack's Relevance

Henry Mack was remarkable not only for his versatility but also for the success he achieved in each of his endeavors. He succeeded in the mercantile trade but also played a vital role in the advancement of his religion and his hometown into the modern world. His achievements were all the more impressive in that they were made in the face of nineteenth-century prejudices. Because Henry Mack was in many ways representative of the mid-nineteenth-century Jew, and because he often found himself at the hub of important events that affected his faith, his biography resembles a portrait of American Jewry in the nineteenth century and the age in which they lived.

Author's note: Earlier versions of this biographical sketch were published in the 1995 issue of <u>American Jewish Archives Journal</u> and the 2003 issue of <u>Stammbaum</u>.

Notes

1. *New York Herald-Tribune*, October 20, 1888.
2. Richard Roy Barrett, "The Institutional Influence of the Jews in Cincinnati," *The American Israelite*, August 28, 1902, 1.
3. William Stern, "On the Fascination of Jewish Surnames," *Yearbook of the Leo Beck Institute* 19, no. 1 (January 1974): 219.
4. Michael W. Rich, "The Mack Family Tree" (unpublished).
5. Marion A. Kaplan, *Jewish Daily Life in Germany, 1618-1945* (New York: Oxford University Press, 2005), 109-110.
6. Werner Eugen Mosse, *Revolution and Evolution, 1848 in German-Jewish History* (Tuebingen, Germany: Mohr Siebeck, 1981), 84.
7. Klaus Guth and Eva Groiss-Lau, *Juedisches Leben auf dem Dorf* (Petersberg, Germany: Michael Imhof Verlag, 1999) [translated into English by Jack C. Heiman in 2002].
8. Franz Zenk, Speech at the Dedication of the Holocaust Monument on the Demmelsdorf-Zeckendorf Highway on July 14, 1991, translation stored in the American Jewish Archives.
9. Selma Stern-Taeubler, "The Motivation of the German-Jewish Emigration to America in the Post-Mendelssohnian Era," in *Essays in American Jewish History*, ed. Jacob Rader Marcus (Cincinnati: American Jewish Archives, 1958), 255.
10. Rudolf Glanz, "The Immigration of German Jews up to 1880," *Studies in Judaica Americana* (New York: Ktav, 1970), 91–92.
11. Guth and Groiss-Lau.
12. Loc. cit.
13. Kaplan, *Jewish Daily Life*, 108.
14. Louis Stix, *Reminiscences Chronicled as a Recreation in His Later Years: 1821–1902* (copy stored in the American Jewish Archives in Cincinnati, Ohio), 16.
15. Birth Registry for the Jewish Community of Demmelsdorf, Bavaria, 1814-1875, stored in The Central Archives of the Jewish People in Jerusalem, Israel.
16. Guth and Groiss-Lau.
17. Loc. cit.
18. Louis Stix, *Reminiscences*, 13.
19. Guth and Groiss-Lau.
20. Louis Stix, *Reminiscences*, 16.
21. Siegfried Rudolph, History of the Jewish Communities in Upper Franconia, translated into English by Elizabeth Petuchowski, stored in the American Jewish Archives.
22. *The Biographical Encyclopedia of Ohio of the Nineteenth Century* (Cincinnati: Galaxy Publishing Co., 1876), s.v. "Henry Mack," 186.
23. Hasia R. Diner, *The Jewish People in America*. Vol.2, *A Time for Gathering: The Second Migration* (Baltimore: Johns Hopkins University Press, 1992), 11.
24. Ibid., 11-13.
25. "The 'Edict of June 10,1813 Regarding the Status of Persons of Jewish Faith in the Kingdom of Bavaria'" by Eric G. Yondorf on the Rijo Research website at www.rijo-research.de

26. H. G. Reissner, "The German-American Jews (1800-1850)," *Yearbook of the Leo Baeck Institute*, 10, no. 1 (January 1965): 69–70.
27. Stern-Taeubler, "Motivation of the German-Jewish Emigration," 253.
28. Louis Stix, *Reminiscences*, 20.
29. Stern-Taeubler, "Motivation of the German-Jewish Emigration," 253–257.
30. Glanz, "Immigration of German Jews," 89–92.
31. *Biographical Encyclopedia of Ohio*, 186.
32. Louis Stix, "Louis Stix: Reminiscences Chronicled as a Recreation in His Later Years: 1821–1902," in *Memoirs of American Jews: 1775–1865*, ed. Jacob Rader Marcus (Philadelphia: Jewish Publication Society, 1955), 312.
33. James Landy, *Cincinnati, Past and Present* (Cincinnati: M. Joblin & Co., 1872), s.v. "Henry Mack," 401-402.
34. Stix, "Louis Stix," 312.
35. Steven G. Mostov, "Dun and Bradstreet Reports as a Source of Jewish Economic History: Cincinnati, 1840–1875," *American Jewish History* 72, no. 3 (March 1983): 340–341.
36. Charles Cist, *Cincinnati in 1841: its Early Annals and Future Prospects* (Cincinnati: Charles Cist, 1841), 37-39, 93-95.
37. Reissner, "German American Jews," 72.
38. Jonathan D. Sarna and Nancy H. Klein, *The Jews of Cincinnati* (Cincinnati: Center for the Study of the American Jewish Experience, 1989), 2.
39. Ibid., 3.
40. Stix, "Louis Stix," 312-313.
41. Nickerdown (pseudonym for Dr. Julius Wise, editor of *The Chicago Israelite*), *The American Israelite*, September 24, 1896, 4.
42. Stix, "Louis Stix," 312-313.
43. Stuart Flexner and Doris Flexner, *The Pessimist's Guide to History* (New York: Avon Books, 1992), 119.
44. Stix, "Louis Stix," 312–313.
45. *Biographical Encyclopedia of Ohio*, 186.
46. Stix, "Louis Stix," 314.
47. Application for U.S. Passport in 1845.
48. Lois E. Hughes, *Citizenship Records Abstracts from Hamilton County, Ohio: 1837–1916* (Bowie, Md.: Heritage Books, 1991), 276.
49. *Biographical Encyclopedia of Ohio*, 186.
50. Henry Mack, "Incidents of Masonic Intercourse in Europe," *Masonic Voice Review* 2, ed. C. Moore (Cincinnati: J. Ernst, 1847): 161-163.
51. Ibid.
52. *Biographical Encyclopedia of Ohio*, loc. cit.
53. Manifest for the ship *Iows* on September 12, 1845.
54. "Golden Wedding," *The American Israelite*, September 10, 1896, 6.
55. Manifest for the ship *Francis Depau* on August 1, 1846.
56. "Golden Wedding."
57. Hamilton County Marriage Records, Microfilm Collection, Western Reserve Historical Society Library, Cleveland.
58. Michael W. Rich, "The Mack Family Tree" (unpublished).
59. *Biographical Encyclopedia of Ohio*, loc. cit.
60. Ira A. Glazier, *Germans to America* (Wilmington, Delaware: Scholarly Resources Inc.).
61. Landy, *Cincinnati, Past and Present*, 401-402.
62. *Directory for the City of Columbus, For the Years 1850-51* (Columbus, Ohio: E. Glover and Wm. Henderson, 1850), 155.
63. Dun and Bradstreet Reports, collection in the Baker Library of Harvard University, Cambridge,

Mass., Vol. 78, 381.
64. Mostov, "Dun and Bradstreet Reports," 341–342.
65. Reissner, "German American Jews," 74–75.
66. Allan Tarshish, "The Economic Life of the American Jew," in *Essays in AmericanJewish History*, ed. Jacob Rader Marcus (Cincinnati: American Jewish Archives, 1958), 279–280.
67. Sarna and Klein, *Jews of Cincinnati*, 38.
68. Department of Commerce, *The Men's Factory-Made Clothing Industry: Report on the Cost of Production of Men's Factory-Made Clothing in the United States* (Washington: Government Printing Office, 1916), 9-11.
69. Ibid.
70. Ibid.
71. Charles Cist, *Sketches and Statistics of Cincinnati in 1859* (Cincinnati: Publisher Unknown, 1859), 271, 341-344, 363-364.
72. Dun and Bradstreet Reports, Vol. 79, 77.
73. Loc. cit.
74. Application for U.S. Passport in 1858.
75. "Last Will and Testament of Abraham Mack," May 8, 1858 (courtesy of Patricia Sutkin).
76. "Whitesboro, NY Train Wreck May 12, 1858: Dreadful Railroad Accident!," *The Erie Observer* (Pennsylvania), May 15, 1858.
77. "The Central Railroad Disaster: Full List of the Names of the Sufferers," *The New York Times*, May 13, 1858.
78. *Annual Report of the New York Central Railroad Company, for the Year Ending September 30th, 1858* (Albany: Weed, Parsons and Company, 1858), 30-33.
79. Henry Mack, "Letter from one of the Sufferers by the Central Railroad Accident," *The New York Times*, June 12, 1858.
80. *The Israelite*, March 22, 1861.
81. *The Israelite*, April 5, 1861.
82. Jonathan Pereira, M.D., *The Elements of Materia Medica and Therapeutics*, Vol. 1, (London: Longman, Brown, Green, and Longmans, 1842), 88-89.
83. Adam Mendelsohn, "Beyond the Battlefield: Reevaluating the Legacy of the Civil War for American Jews," *American Jewish Archives Journal* 64. Nos. 1 and 2 (2012): 82-111.
84. Shelley R. Slade and Brad Leneis, "Congressman Charles H. Van Wyck: Anti-Fraud Warrior of the 37th Congress" on the Vogel, Slade & Goldstein, LLP website at www.vsg-law.org; Mark Greenbaum, "The Civil War's War on Fraud," *The New York Times*, March 7, 2013.
85. Ibid.
86. Ibid.
87. Ibid.
88. Alfred E. Lee, *History of the City of Columbus, Capital of Ohio* (New York: Munsell & Co., 1892), Vol. 2, 92-93.
89. Mark R. Wilson, *The Business of Civil War: Military Mobilization and the State, 1861-1865* (Baltimore, Maryland: Johns Hopkins University Press, 2006), 215.
90. Mendelsohn, 95.
91. "The War in Western Virginia," *Daily Intelligencer* (Wheeling, Virginia), September 26, 1861, 2.
92. *Reports of the Committees of the House of Representatives made during the Second Session of the Thirty-Seventh Congress. 1861-'62* (Washington, D.C.: Government Printing Office, 1862), 745.
93. Ibid., 917-926.
94. Ibid., 766.
95. "Clothing for the Army of the Union," *American Jewish Archives Journal* 13, no. 2 (November 1961): 174–175.
96. Mark R. Wilson, "Table B6: Leading Clothing Suppliers to the U.S. Army, 1861-1864," *The

Business of Civil War, 235.
97. Dun and Bradstreet Reports, Vol. 79, 123 and Vol. 84, 174.
98. "'Dr. Lewis Adolphus'—an English Schoolmaster and his Operations in America," *American Educational Monthly* 1 (New York: Schermerhorn, Bancroft & Co., 1864): 109.
99. "Leonard W. Mack v. Charles Fries" in *Reprint of Ohio Cases Published in Fifteen Volumes, American Law Record, 1872-1887*, Vol. 1 (Norwalk, Ohio: The Laning Printing Company, 1897), 174-180.
100. E. L. DeWitt, "Fries v. Mack" in *Reports of Cases Argued and Determined in the Supreme Court Commission of Ohio*, Vol. 33 (Cincinnati, Ohio: Robert Clarke & Co., 1879), 52-62.
101. Clarence D. Long, "Table 14: Annual Earnings," *Wages and Earnings in the United States, 1860-1890* (Princeton University Press, 1960), 42.
102. Reports of Committees, 991-993.
103. Ibid., 1050-1076.
104. Ibid.
105. Ibid., 917-926.
106. Ibid., 926-930.
107. Ibid., 917-926.
108. "More Indictments by the United States Grand Jury," *The Cincinnati Enquirer*, April 30, 1862, 3.
109. "The Lowenstein Embezzlement Case Before the United States Court," *The Cincinnati Enquirer*, May 1, 1862, 3.
110. John Boh, Local Civil War Supply Lines, *Bulletin of the Kenton County Historical Society* (September/October 2012), 1-10.
111. *The Business of the Civil War*, 235.
112. "Home News. Internal Revenue. Returns of Dealers' Sales, First District, for 1867-68," *Cincinnati Daily Gazette*, May 16, 1868.
113. "Business of Cincinnati. Internal Revenue Returns for 1868. The First District," *Cincinnati Daily Gazette*, January 19, 1869.
114. "Internal Revenue Returns," *Cincinnati Daily Gazette*, November 2, 1870.
115. Cincinnati City Directories, collection in Western Reserve Historical Society, Cleveland.
116. *The Israelite*, September 7 and 28, 1866.
117. "A Big Fire in Cincinnati: Two Clothing Houses Burned, Involving a Loss of $635,000," *The New York Times*, November 21, 1886.
118. D. J. Kenny, *Illustrated Cincinnati: A Hand-Book of the Queen City* (Cincinnati: Robert Clarke & Co., 1875), 224.
119. Ibid., 36.
120. Dun and Bradstreet, Vol. 64, 174.
121. United States Census.
122. Dun and Bradstreet, Vol. 2, 123.
123. United States Census.
124. Sidney D. Maxwell, *History of the Exposition of Textile Fabrics: Held in Cincinnati, August 3rd, 4th, 5th, 6th, and 7th 1869* (Cincinnati: Gazette Co.).
125. Benjamin F. Lyle, M.D., "Points on Smallpox," *The Cincinnati Lancet-Clinic* 43 (July 8, 1899): 25-32.
126. "Small-Pox in Cincinnati. Spread of the Disease – Outcry Against the Health Board," *The New York Times*, May 6, 1882.
127. "The Board of Health. The Attempts of Other Cities to Injure Cincinnati's Trade," *Cincinnati Daily Gazette*, May 26, 1882.
128. Cincinnati City Directories.
129. Ibid.
130. *The Clothier and Furnisher* 14, no. 6 (January 1885) (New York: L.D. Gallison): 56.

131. "Strike Situation," *Cincinnati Post*, May 11, 1886.
132. "A Big Fire in Cincinnati," *The New York Times*.
133. "What is One Man's Loss is Another's Gain," *The Wichita (Kansas) Daily Eagle*, November 10, 1895, 6.
134. "City Briefs," *Cincinnati Post*, August 15, 1895.
135. Cincinnati City Directories.
136. Dun and Bradstreet Reports, Vol. 79, 77.
137. Morris U. Schappes, ed., *A Documentary History of the Jews in the United States, 1654–1875* (New York: Citadel Press, 1950), 472–476.
138. Ibid.
139. Ibid.
140. Joakim Isaacs, "Candidate Grant and the Jews," *American Jewish Archives Journal* 17, no. 1 (April 1965): 8.
141. Ibid., 8–9.
142. Schappes, *Documentary History*, loc. cit.
143. Bruce Catton, *This Hallowed Ground* (New York: Washington Square Press, 1961), 270-271.
144. "The Grant Family's Cotton Speculations: Official Record of the GrantMack Cotton Case in 1862," *New York Daily Tribune*, September 19, 1872.
145. *Democratic Speaker's Hand-Book: Containing Every Thing Necessary for the Defense of the National Democracy in the Coming Presidential Campaign*, compiled by Matthew Carey, Jr. (Cincinnati, Ohio: Miami Printing and Publishing Company, 1868), 42-43.
146. Isaacs, "Candidate Grant," 9.
147. Bertram Wallace Korn, *American Jewry and the Civil War* (Philadelphia: Jewish Publication Society, 1951), 138–147.
148. John Y. Simon, ed., *The Papers of Ulysses S. Grant*, Vol. 19: July 1, 1868 – October 31, 1869 (Southern Illinois University Press, 1995), 25-28.
149. Bernard Martin, *A History of Judaism*, Vol. 2 (New York: Basic Books, 1974), 286–318.
150. Guth and Groiss-Lau.
151. James Gutheim Heller, *Isaac M. Wise: His Life, Work and Thought* (New York: Union of American Hebrew Congregations, 1965), 244–245.
152. Sarna and Klein, *Jews of Cincinnati*, 48.
153 Martin, History of Judaism, 305.
154. Charles Frederic Goss, *Cincinnati: The Queen City, 1788–1912* (Cincinnati: S. J. Clarke, 1912), 31–32.
155. Isaac M. Wise Temple Trustees, *The History of the K. K. Bene Yeshurun, of Cincinnati, Ohio, from the Date of its Organization* (Cincinnati: Bloch Printing Co., 1892).
156. *The Israelite*, September 28, 1866.
157. Trustees, *The History of the K. K. Bene Yeshurun*.
158. *The Occident*, July 1852.
159. Trustees, *The History of the K. K. Bene Yeshurun*.
160. *The American Israelite*, November 25, 1859.
161. Ibid., January 27, 1860.
162. *The Occident*, July 1852.
163. *The American Israelite*, January 27, 1860.
164. Stephan F. Brumberg, "The Cincinnati Bible War (1869-1873) and its Impact on the Education of the City's Protestants, Catholics, and Jews," *American Jewish Archives Journal* 54, no. 2 (2002): 11-46.
165. "Celebration of the Tenth Anniversary of the Talmud Yelodim Institute," *The Penny Press* (Cincinnati), January 27, 1860.
166. *The Israelite*, November 16, 1860.
167. Ibid., January 23, 1863.

168. Ibid., October 2, 1863.
169. Ann Deborah Michael, "The Origins of the Jewish Community of Cincinnati, 1817–1860," *Cincinnati Historical Society Bulletin* 30, nos. 3 and 4 (Fall-Winter 1972): 168–169.
170. Goss, *Cincinnati*, 42–43.
171. Charles Theodore Greve, ed., *Centennial History of Cincinnati and Representative Citizens* (Chicago: Biographical Publishing Co., 1904), s.v. "Hon. Henry Mack," p. 233.
172. Brumberg, "The Cincinnati Bible War."
173. Betsy Will, Congregational Life and Activities in the Postbellum Period, 1866-1881, as Reflected in the Records of Congregation B'nai Jeshurun, Cincinnati (unpublished manuscript, 1987), stored in the American Jewish Archives in Cincinnati, Ohio.
174. Heller, *Isaac M. Wise*, 246–247.
175. Ibid., 235–239.
176. Ibid., 273–282.
177. Schappes, *Documentary History*, 392–394, 677–678.
178. Heller, *Isaac M. Wise*, 375–379.
179. Goss, *Cincinnati*, 32–33.
180. *The Israelite*, April 10, 1863.
181. Ibid., May 15, 1863.
182. Ibid., September 28, 1866.
183. Ibid., October 26, 1866.
184. Ibid., December 28, 1866.
185. "The Jewish Temple – Extraordinary Sale of Pews," *The Evansville* (Indiana) *Journal*, September 1, 1866, 2.
186. Walter J. Daley, "The Black Cholera Comes to the Central Valley of America in the 19th Century – 1832, 1849, and Later," *Transactions of the American Clinical and Climatological Association* 119 (2008): 143-153.
187. "The Jewish Burial Grounds," *The Israelite*, July 15, 1870, 9.
188. International Jewish Cemetery Project on the Jewish Genealogy website.
189. Sarna and Klein, *Jews of Cincinnati*, 46.
190. Find a Grave website.
191. Goss, *Cincinnati*, 51.
192. Diner, *A Time for Gathering*, 93.
193. "America's First Jewish Hospital," *Significant Documents Illuminating the American Jewish Experience*, American Jewish Archives.
194. "Domestic Record," *The Israelite*, April 20, 1860, 331.
195. *The Israelite*, July 16, 1858, 15.
196. *Annual Message of the Mayor of Cincinnati to the Common Council. April, 1878* (Cincinnati: Times Book and Job Printing Establishment, 1878), 70.
197. "Congregation Revealed As Center of Early Reform Efforts in America," *The American Israelite*, December 8, 1932, A1.
198. Gotthard Deutsch, "Dr. Abraham Bettmann, A Pioneer Physician of Cincinnati," *American Jewish Historical Quarterly* 23 (1915): 112.
199. Will, *Congregational Life*.
200. Greve, *Centennial History of Cincinnati*, 233.
201. *The Occident*, March 1848.
202. Trustees, *The History of the K. K. Bene Yeshurun*.
203. Heller, *Isaac M. Wise*, 408–414.
204. Diner, *Time for Gathering*, 222.
205. Heller, loc. cit.
206. *Proceedings of the Union of American Hebrew Congregations* 1 (1873-1879) (Cincinnati: Bloch & Co., Printers): i-xiii.

207. Ibid., 20.
208. Ibid., 142-144.
209. Debra R. Blank, "History of Confirmation" in *Life Cycles in Jewish and Christian Worship* (Notre Dame, Indiana: The University of Notre Dame Press, 1996).
210. *The New York Times*, July 23, 1874.
211. *Proceedings of the Union*, 123 and 144.
212. Ibid., 225.
213. David Philipson, "History of the Hebrew Union College, 1875–1925," *Hebrew Union College Jubilee Volume* (Cincinnati, 1925), 13–16.
214. Irving Aaron Mandel, "Attitude of the American Jewish Community Toward East-European Immigration: As Reflected in the Anglo-Jewish Press (1880-1890)," *American Jewish Archives Journal* 3, no. 1 (June 1950): 11-36.
215. Ibid.
216. Ibid.
217. Ibid.
218. *The San Antonio, Texas Evening Light*, June 12, 1882.
219. Mandel, "East –European Immigration," 11-36.
220. Daniel J. Ryan, "Lincoln and Ohio," *Ohio History* 32, 69-74.
221. *Address by Abraham Lincoln of Illinois in Cincinnati, Ohio September 17, 1859* (Cincinnati, Ohio: Chas. F. Lots Printing and Stationary Co., 1910).
222. *Biographical Encyclopedia of Ohio*, 186.
223. Cincinnati City Directories.
224. John H. White, Jr., "Horsecars: City Transit Before the Age of Electricity." on webpage at http://spec.lib.miamioh.edu/wp-content/uploads/2013/02/Horse-Car-brochure-for-website.pdf
225. Ibid.
226. Ibid.
227. *Laws and General Ordinances of the City of Cincinnati*, compiled by William Disney (Cincinnati: Robert Clarke & Co., 1866), 720-762.
228. "The Reports of the Investigating Committee," *The Cincinnati Penny Press*, December 8, 1859.
229. "The Investigation of Bribery and Corruption of Office in the City Council," *The Cincinnati Enquirer*, December 18, 1859, 3.
230. "Attempt to Buy up a Councilman," *Wheeling* (West Virginia) *Daily Intelligencer*, September 7, 1859.
231. Donald A. Hutslar, "'God's Scourge': The Cholera Years in Ohio," *Ohio History* 105 (Summer-Autumn 1996): 174-191.
232. *Biographical Encyclopedia of Ohio*, 186.
233. Hutslar, "God's Scourge," 232.
234. *Henry Mack, Report on Sewers & Drainage: Presented to the City Council, July 11th, 1860* (Cincinnati: Gazette Co., 1860), 1-8.
235. R. C. Phillips, *Map of Cincinnati* (New York: H. H. Lloyd & Co., 1874), 55.
236. Jon Roberts, "Garbage: The Black Sheep of the Family. A Brief History of Waste Regulation in the United States and Oklahoma," Oklahoma Department of Environmental Quality website at www.deq.state.ok.us
237. *Cincinnati Daily Press*, April 7, 1860.
238. "Contractor and Street Cleaning – Condition of the Streets," *Cincinnati Daily Press*, May 28, 1860.
239. "Mayor's Proclamation," *Cincinnati Daily Press*, October 16, 1860.
240. *Cincinnati Daily Press*, July 19, 1860.
241. "The Reception Ball in Honor of the Prince of Wales," *Cincinnati Daily Press*, September 28,1860.
242. "Editorial Article," *The American Israelite*, November 12, 1880.

243. "Henry Mack to Abraham Lincoln," handwritten letter dated February 15, 1861. The Papers of Abraham Lincoln on webpage at http://lincolnpapers2.dataformat.com/images/1861/02/257431.pdf
244. "Demmelsdorf" on the Allemmania-Judaica website.
245. *Biographical Encyclopedia of Ohio*, 187.
246. "County Military Committee" in *History of Clark County* (Chicago: W.H. Beers & Co., 1881), 297.
247. "Cuyahoga County Military Committee" in The Encyclopedia of Cleveland History on the website at www.ech.case.edu
248. Joseph E. Holliday, "Relief for Soldiers' Families in Ohio during the Civil War," *Ohio History* 71 (July 1962): 97-112.
249. "County Military Committee", loc. cit.
250. "Cuyahoga County Military Committee", loc. cit.
251. Holliday, loc. cit.
252. Holliday, loc. cit.
253. "County Military Committee", loc. cit.
254. "Cuyahoga County Military Committee", loc. cit.
255. *Biographical Encyclopedia of Ohio*, 187.
256. "Reception Committee," *The Cincinnati Enquirer*, September 8, 1866, 2.
257. Schappes, *Documentary History*, 719.
258. *Annual Report of the Board of Trustees of The Public Library of Cincinnati, Ohio for the Year Ending June 30, 1899* (Cincinnati: Press of C. J. Krehbiel & Co., 1899), 30-32, 45, 134.
259. Goss, *Cincinnati*, 231.
260. Greve, *Centennial History of Cincinnati*, 233.
261. *Annual Report of the Board*, 44-45.
262. Ibid., 43-46.
263. Ibid., 45.
264. Henry Mack, "Final Report of the Building Committee on Public Library Building, and Historical Facts Connected with the Same," handwritten manuscript stored in the Public Library of Cincinnati and Hamilton County.
265. Brumberg, "The Cincinnati Bible War."
266. Schappes, *Documentary History*, 520–537, 719–723.
267. Landy, *Cincinnati, Past and Present*, 404.
268. *Common Schools of Cincinnati: Annual Reports and Handbooks* (Cincinnati: Ohio Valley Publishing and Manufacturing Co.).
269. Brumberg, "The Cincinnati Bible War," 12-13.
270. "The New School Board Organization Yesterday Afternoon," *Cincinnati Daily Enquirer*, July 3, 1872.
271. *Cincinnati Daily Enquirer*, April 8, 1874.
272. "The Eighteenth Ward Representation in the Board of Education," *Cincinnati Commercial Tribune*, March 28, 1875.
273. *Cincinnati Daily Times*, August 3, 1875.
274. "Board of Trade Annual," *Cincinnati Commercial Tribune*, March 2, 1876.
275. "Board of Transportation," *Cincinnati Daily Times*, January 28, 1876.
276. "Board of Transportation," *Cincinnati Daily Times*, June 1, 1876.
277. "Society for the Preservation of Music Hall" website.
278. "Cincinnati Music Hall," *Cincinnati Daily Gazette*, December 9, 1875.
279. "Music Hall Incorporators," *Cincinnati Daily Times*, December 13, 1875.
280. "The New Halls. The Committee at Work in Earnest," *Cincinnati Daily Gazette*, June 15, 1875.
281. "The Celebrated Cotton Transactions of Henry Mack with Jesse R. Grant – The Price of Blood," *Cincinnati Daily Enquirer*, October 1, 1869.

282. "The Ring Ticket – Antecedents of Its Candidates," *Cincinnati Daily Enquirer*, October 3, 1869.
283. "Grant and His Gold Speculations," *Cincinnati Daily Enquirer*, October 7, 1869.
284. "Henry Mack, Esq.," *Cincinnati Commercial Tribune*, October 10, 1869.
285. "Columbus News," *Cincinnati Daily Gazette*, October 23, 1869.
286. "Chronicling America: Historic American Newspapers," Library of Congress website.
287. "Our New Postmaster. How it happened," *Cincinnati Commercial Tribune*, December 18, 1873.
288. "The *Cincinnati Post* Office," *New York Herald*, December 18, 1873.
289. "The June Convention," *The Cincinnati Daily Star*, February 28, 1876.
290. *Proceedings of the Republican National Convention, Held at Cincinnati, Ohio, Wednesday, Thursday, and Friday, June 14, 15, and 16, 1876.*
291. *Decatur* (Illinois) *Daily Republican*, November 3, 1876.
292. "The Disputed Election of 1876" on the American Experience website at www.pbs.org
293. "Let Us Have Peace. A Petition from Representative Cincinnatians," *The Cincinnati Daily Star*, January 5, 1877.
294. "Let Us Have Peace. The Business Men of Cincinnati on the Vexed Question," *The Cincinnati Daily Star*, February 23, 1877.
295. C. Vann Woodward, *Reunion and Reaction: The Compromise of 1877 and the End of Reconstruction* (New York: Oxford University Press, 1951).
296. Todd Arrington, "Exodusters – Homestead National Monument of America," on the U.S. National Park Services website at www.nps.gov
297. "The Colored Refugees. Action Taken for Their Relief," *The Cincinnati Daily Star*, May 20, 1879.
298. *The American Israelite*, September 30, 1887, 6.
299. "Off They Go! Hamilton's Legislators Start for Columbus," *Cincinnati Post*, December 29, 1887.
300. "The Caucus Undone," *Cincinnati Commercial Tribune*, January 3, 1888.
301. "Senator Mack at Work. He Gets Two Bills Through the Senate and Introduces Another," *Cincinnati Commercial Tribune*, January 28, 1888.
302. "Glad They are Home," *Cincinnati Post*, April 18, 1889.
303. "Dow Law," Ohio History Central website of the Ohio Historical Society.
304. Ibid.
305. "Local Option. The Township Bill Relieved of the Two Mile Restriction," *Cincinnati Commercial Tribune*, March 1, 1888.
306. "Two Cent Fares. The House Amends the Haley Bill and Passes It. The Temperance Instruction Bill Passes the Senate," *Canton Repository*, April 6, 1888.
307. "Anti-Saloon Basis," *Cincinnati Post*, March 7, 1888.
308. Protective Association," *Cincinnati Commercial Tribune*, April 7, 1888.
309. "Anti-Saloon Basis," *Cincinnati Post*, March 7, 1888.
310. "'It Would be Robbery', Says Senator Mack, 'For the State to Take Any of the Dow tax,'" *Cincinnati Post*, March 7, 1888.
311. "Protective Association," *Cincinnati Commercial Tribune*, April 7, 1888.
312. "Hard on Hamilton. The Owen Sunday Closing Bill Becomes Law," *Cleveland Plain Dealer*, April 14, 1888.
313. "The Dow Law. Another Important Amendment Passes the House," *Canton Repository*, March 8, 1888.
314. "Put on Record. The Republicans Opposed to the Sunday Closing Bill," *Cleveland Plain Dealer*, April 7, 1888.
315. "Hard on Hamilton. The Owen Sunday Closing Bill Becomes Law," *Cleveland Plain Dealer*, April 14, 1888.
316. "Protective Association," *Cincinnati Commercial Tribune*, April 7, 1888.

317. "$3,085,000. Total Appropriations of the Present Legislature," *Cincinnati Commercial Tribune*, April 13, 1888.
318. "Hard on Hamilton. The Owen Sunday Closing Bill Becomes Law," *Cleveland Plain Dealer*, April 14, 1888.
319. "Put on Record. The Republicans Opposed to the Sunday Closing Bill," *Cleveland Plain Dealer*, April 7, 1888.
320. "Many Amendments," *Cleveland Plain Dealer*, April 6, 1888.
321. "Sunday Closing. The Owen Bill Passes the Senate and is a Law. Seventeen Republicans and Eight Democrats Vote Yes. The Hamilton County Members Do Not Vote, Though Mack Makes a Strong Speech Against the Measure," *Cincinnati Commercial Tribune*, April 14, 1888.
322. *The American Israelite*, June 22, 1888.
323. *American Jewish Year Book* (Philadelphia: The Jewish Publication Society of America, 1899), 283-284.
324. Janice Rothschild Blumberg, "Voices for Justice: Jacob M. Rothschild in Atlanta (1946-1973) and Edward B.M. Browne in New York (1881-1889)" (unpublished).
325. Ibid.
326. Ibid.
327. *Knoxville Daily Journal and Tribune*, October 5, 1888.
328. "A Prominent Hebrew to Take the Stump," *New York Herald-Tribune*, October 20, 1888.
329. Letter written to Henry Mack by Benjamin Harrison, November 16, 1888, stored in American Jewish Archives, Cincinnati, Ohio.
330. Letter written to Benjamin Harrison by Rabbi Edward Benjamin Morris Browne, November 16, 1888, stored in American Jewish Archives, Cincinnati, Ohio.
331. Ibid.
332. Letter written to Henry Mack.
333. "Two Senatorial Visitors," *Cleveland Plain Dealer*, January 4, 1889.
334. "Local Inklings," *Cincinnati Post*, December 2, 1889.
335. "Federal Persimmons," *Cincinnati Post*, March 5, 1889.
336. Greve, loc. cit.
337. "The Board of Trustees and the Administration of Their Trust," by H.P. Boyden in *The Cincinnati Southern Railway: A History* (Cincinnati, Ohio, 1902), 36-37.
338. *History of Cincinnati and Hamilton County, Their Past and Present* (Cincinnati, Ohio: S.B. Nelson & Co., 1894), 296-297.
339. Scott R. Fletcher, "Public Dreams, Private Means: Cincinnati and its Southern Railway, 1869-1901," *Journal of Transport History* 24 (March 2003): 38-58.
340. "Railroad Trustees," *The Cincinnati Enquirer*, June 30, 1869, 8.
341. "The Building of the Road," by Colonel George B. Nicholson in *The Cincinnati Southern Railway: A History* (Cincinnati, Ohio, 1902), 49-55.
342. Henry Paine Boyden, *The Beginnings of the Cincinnati Southern Railway: A Sketch of the Years, 1869-1878* (Cincinnati: The Robert Clarke Company, 1901), 57.
343. "People & Events: The Panic of 1873" on the American Experience website at www.pbs.org
344. Boyden, *The Beginnings of the Cincinnati Southern Railway*, 44.
345. Ibid., 57.
346. Ibid., 82.
347. Ibid., 57.
348. "Mack's Mind. He Speaks it Freely About Trustee Schiff. Also an Allusion to a Gentleman of the Name Ferguson," *The Cincinnati Enquirer*, July 13, 1877, 8.
349. Ibid.
350. "The C.S.R.R. Trustees. A Nice Little Row In the Camp," *The Cincinnati Enquirer*, June 28, 1877, 2.
351. Ibid.

352. "Mack's Mind," *The Cincinnati Enquirer*.
353. "The Building of the Road," loc. cit.
354. E.A. Ferguson, *Founding of the Cincinnati Southern Railway with an Autobiographical Sketch* (Cincinnati: The Robert Clarke Co., 1905), 100-104.
355. Fletcher, "Public Dreams."
356. "The Road Under Lease," in *The Cincinnati Southern Railway: A History*, 56-65.
357. Boyden, *The Beginnings of the Cincinnati Southern Railway*, 68.
358. Ibid., 76.
359. Fletcher, "Public Dreams," 57.
360. Boyden, *The Beginnings of the Cincinnati Southern Railway*, 81-82.
361. Boyden, *The Beginnings of the Cincinnati Southern Railway*, 57 and 82-83.
362. "Leonard W. Mack v. Charles Fries," 180.
363. DeWitt, "Fries v. Mack," 56.
364. "Presidential Party. Excursion Over the Cincinnati Southern," *Cincinnati Commercial Tribune*, September 13, 1879.
365. "The Excursion Over the Cincinnati Southern. The First Through Train. Reception of the Visitors in Chattanooga. Interview with Trustee Henry Mack," *Cincinnati Commercial Tribune*, December 22, 1879.
366. Cincinnati Southern Railway website at www.cincinnatisouthernrailway.org
367. "The Road Under Lease," loc. cit.
368. "A History of The Chattanooga Choo-Choo Terminal Station & Trolley," by Daniel Towers Lewis (Chattanooga, Tennessee: The Simon Moon Historical Society, 2002).
369. J.H. Hollander, *The Cincinnati Southern Railway: A Study in Municipal Activity* (Baltimore: The Johns Hopkins Press, 1894), 50-59.
370. *Moody's Manual of Investment: American and Foreign*, Vol. 3, ed. John Sherman Porter (New York: Analyses Publishing Co., 1912), 154.
371. "The Cincinnati Southern," *Memphis Daily Appeal*, October 9, 1881, 4.
372. *The American Israelite*, October 21, 1881.
373. J.H. Hollander, loc. cit.
374. "State Capital," *Cincinnati Commercial Tribune*, January 8, 1880.
375. *The Evening Bulletin* [Maysville, Kentucky], March 8, 1888, 1.
376. "Queen and Crescent," *The American Israelite*, March 30, 1888, 6.
377. "En Route to New Orleans: The Legislative Junketers Connect on That Free Ride," *Springfield* [Ohio] *Daily Republic*, March 17, 1888, 1.
378. Ibid.
379. "They Are Red Hot. Union Labor Party Wants Legal Proceedings Instituted Against the Trustees of the Southern Railway," *Cincinnati Commercial Tribune*, March 17, 1888.
380. *The News-Herald* [Hillsboro, Ohio], February 28, 1889, 2.
381. "A Close Shave. Mack's Southern Railroad Extension Voted On. The Chamber of Commerce Defeats the Releasing Scheme by 390 to 312," *The Cincinnati Enquirer*, February 21, 1889, 8.
382. "State Capital," loc. cit.
383. "The Road Under Lease," loc. cit.
384. "The Southern Railroad. Action on Senator Mack's Bill to Extend Its Lease," *Cincinnati Commercial Tribune*, February 7, 1889.
385. "The Mack Bill. Southern Railroad Lease Extension Before the Chamber of Commerce," *Cincinnati Commercial Tribune*, February 17, 1889.
386. "The Building of the Road," in *The Cincinnati Southern Railway: A History*, 49-55.
387. Dun and Bradstreet Reports, Vol. 83, 314 and Vol. 82, 321.
388. I.J. Benjamin, *Three Years in America* (Philadelphia: Jewish Publication Society, 1956), Vol. 1, 313 and Vol. 2, 278.
389. Nickerdown, loc. cit.

390. Dun and Bradstreet Reports, Vol. 78, 381 and Vol. 79, 77.
391. Mostov, "Dun and Bradstreet Reports," 339.
392. "Jewish Merchants of Cincinnati," *The New York Times*, June 26, 1877.
393. Diner, *Time for Gathering*, 151-152.
394. The Center for Jewish History website at www.jewsinamerica.org
395. Loc. cit.
396. *The Occident*, May 1847, June 1847 and July 1847.
397. Loc. cit.
398. "Incidents of Masonic Intercourse," 161-163.
399. Diner, *Time for Gathering*, 109-113.
400. Sarna and Klein, *Jews of Cincinnati*, 44.
401. Greve, *Centennial History of Cincinnati*, 233.
402. "Joseph Levy, et al. v. B'nai B'rith, et al." in *American Law Record: 1872-1887*, Volume 5 (Norwalk, Ohio: The Laning Printing Company, 1897), 401-402.
403. *The Menorah: A Monthly Magazine, Official Organ of the Independent Order of B'ne B'rith* 25 (New York: Menorah Publishing Company, 1898): 114.
404. *The Menorah* 23: 36.
405. Greve, *Centennial History of Cincinnati*, 233.
406. *Boyd's Hand-Book of Cincinnati* (Cincinnati: Jos. B. Boyd, 1869), 63-72.
407. "Allemania Society – Thirteenth Aniversary [sic]," *Cincinnati Commercial Tribune*, December 8, 1878.
408. "Allemania Society," *Cincinnati Daily Times*, December 8, 1875.
409. "Allemania. Dedication of the New Society Hall," Cincinnati Daily Gazette, May 2, 1879.
410. "The Allemania. Dedication of Their New Quarters Last Night. One of the Most Brilliant Social Events of the Season. Youth, Beauty and Wealth Out in Force," *The Cincinnati Enquirer*, May 2, 1879, 8.
411. Lance J. Sussman, "The Myth of the Trefa Banquet: American Culinary Culture and the Radicalization of Food Policy in American Judaism," *American Jewish Archives Journal* 57, nos. 1 and 2 (2005): 29-52.
412. Richard Rhoda, "Urban Transport and the Expansion of Cincinnati 1858 to 1920," *Cincinnati Historical Society Bulletin* 35, no. 2 (Summer 1977): 130-143.
413. Cincinnati City Directories.
414. Rhoda, "Urban Transport," 131-143.
415. Ibid.
416 Sarna and Klein, *Jews of Cincinnati*, 116–118.
417. Cincinnati City Directories.
418. Rhoda, "Urban Transport."
419. Sarna and Klein, *Jews of Cincinnati*, 116-118.
420. "For Sale – Farms," *Cincinnati Post*, May 11, 1886.
421. Geo. Moessinger and Fred Bertsch, *Map of Hamilton County, Ohio* (Cincinnati, Ohio: Geo. Moessinger & Fred Bertsch, March 1884).
422. Cincinnati City Directories.
423. Conversation with Theodore Mack about information provided by his grandfather Theodore Mack.
424. 1870 and 1880 United States Census.
425. Betty Smiddy, "A Little Piece of Paradise" from the College Hill, Ohio webpage at http://www.collegehill.info/documents/history.pdf
426. Nelson, *History of Cincinnati and Hamilton County*, 418-425.
427. "The Cincinnati Southern," *Cincinnati Commercial Tribune*, July 23, 1878.
428. The Farmers Hotel: Historic Designation Report, prepared by Cincinnati Northside Community Urban Redevelopment Corporation for the City of Cincinnati, April 18, 2013.

429. Ibid.
430. "Local," *The American Israelite*, June 28, 1894, 6.
431. "Local," *The American Israelite*, August 13, 1886, 9.
432. *The American Israelite*, 1889.
433. *Williams' Hamilton County Directory for 1887* (Cincinnati, Ohio: Williams & Co., 1887), 155.
434. "New Narrow-Gauge Railroad Project," *Cincinnati Commercial Tribune*, June 20, 1876.
435. Center for Urban Transportation Research, University of South Florida, Tampa, Florida, "Evaluation of the Economic Viability of Narrow-Gauge Local Rail Systems," 2001.
436. "Narrow-Gauge Railways. What the Proposed System of Lines will be for Cincinnati," *Cincinnati Commercial Tribune*, April 15, 1877.
437. "Narrow-Gauge Railways. Their Development in Southern Ohio During the Last Year," *Cincinnati Daily Gazette*, December 19, 1878.
438. "Sand on the Rail. Trestles and Trucks," *Cincinnati Daily Times*, March 11, 1876.
439. "New Narrow-Gauge Railroad Project," *Cincinnati Commercial Tribune*, June 20, 1876.
440. Ibid.
441. *Annual Report of the Ohio Secretary of State* (Columbus: Nevins & Myers, State Printers, 1878), 122.
442. "Mt. Airy, Venice and Liberty Narrow-Gauge Railroad," *Cincinnati Commercial Tribune*, December 22, 1876.
443. "Important Railroad Meeting. The Mt. Airy, Venice & Liberty Narrow Gauge," *Cincinnati Daily Gazette*, May 1, 1879.
444. "An 'L' Road. College Hill and Mt. Airy Want One," *Cincinnati Post*, November 24, 1887.
445. United States Census Records.
446. Cincinnati City Directories.
447. *Cincinnati Commercial Tribune*, February 3, 1884.
448. Ibid., April 6, 1884.
449. Ibid., February 9, 1890.
450. Ibid., March 16, 1890.
451. "The Railway World," *Cincinnati Commercial Tribune*, November 29, 1881.
452. "American Millionaires: The Tribune's List of all Persons in the United States Reported to Worth a Million or More," *New York Tribune*, June 1892, 41.
453. "CPI Inflation Calculator" on the United States Department of Labor website.
454. United States Census Records.
455. *The Israelite*, November 14, 1862.
456. Ibid., February 12, 1864.
457. United States Census Records.
458. *The Wisconsin Jewish Chronicle* (Milwaukee), September 11, 1938, 2.
459. Find a Grave website.
460. *Germans to America Series II*, Vol. 2 (Wilmington, Delaware: Scholarly Resources, 2002).
461. United States Census Records.
462. Ibid.
463. Isidor Coons, "The Wilkes-Barre, Pennsylvania, Jewish Community: A Resume of the Lives and Activities of the Pioneer Jewish Families and their Descendants from 1838-1951," manuscript stored in the American Jewish Historical Society in New York, New York.
464. "Jewish Race and German Soul": A Re-Evaluation of Ethnic Identity Among Cincinnati's German Jewish Immigrants, 1830-1880 by Christy M. Noneman (unpublished honors thesis for Ball State University in Muncie, Indiana, 1998).
465. Loc. cit.
466. Loc. cit.
467. Loc. cit.
468. United States Census Records.

469. Cincinnati City Directories.
470. Theodore Mack, loc. cit.
471. *The Occident*, December 1849.
472. Loc. cit.
473. Diner, *Time for Gathering*, 212.
474. Ibid, 221-222.
475. "Theodore Mack's Defection," *Cincinnati Commercial Tribune*, September 26, 1885.
476. "Business Not Blood," *Cleveland Plain Dealer*, September 26, 1885.
477. "Birthday Celebration. Notable gathering at the Home of Henry Mack," *Cincinnati Commercial Tribune*, December 25, 1881.
478. "Mt. Airy," *Cincinnati Commercial Tribune*, July 24, 1878.
479. Cincinnati City Directories.
480. "Emil Mack, Son of the Clothier, Wanted for Turning a Trick," *The Cincinnati Enquirer*, February 7, 1894, 5.
481. "Mack Was in Town," *The Cincinnati Enquirer*, February 9, 1894, 8.
482. "Make it Good. Said Bloom to Mack, by Four O'Clock," *Cincinnati Post*, August 9, 1894.
483. "Buried the Hatchet," *The Cincinnati Enquirer*, August 11, 1894, 16.
484. "The Last Will and Testament of Henry Mack," Hamilton County Ohio Wills, 1791-1901 Collection, stored in the Archives and Rare Books Library of the University of Cincinnati.
485. "Sad Errand. Alfred Mack Returned With Brother's Body," *Cincinnati Post*, September 19, 1898.
486. From an annotation in Henry's Bible (courtesy of Theodore Mack).
487. Application for U.S. Passport by Henry Mack on May 23, 1888.
488. *The American Israelite*, January 19, 1899, 5.
489. Oil portrait of Henry Mack (courtesy of Theodore Mack).
490. *The American Israelite*, August 17, 1893, 6.
491. *The American Israelite*, February 13, 1896, 6.
492. "Hon. Henry Mack, Seriously Ill at His Home, Grave Fears For His Recovery Entertained – An Active and Honorable Career," *The Cincinnati Enquirer*, June 28, 1896, 12.
493. "Golden Sands," *Cincinnati Post*, September 15, 1896.
494. Will N. Friend, "Golden Wedding," *The American Israelite*, September 17, 1896, 6.
495. "A Happy Couple They," *Kentucky Post*, September 11, 1896, 6.
496. From an insurance policy questionnaire filled out by Henry Mack's grandson Murray Newburgh (courtesy of Michael W. Rich).
497. "Henry Mack Better," *The Cincinnati Enquirer*, December, 16, 1896, 12.
498. Henry Mack's Death Certificate, stored in the Hamilton County Probate Court in Cincinnati, Ohio.
499. "Death of Henry Mack," *The American Israelite*, December 31, 1896, 6.
500. "Verified. The Strange Prophesy Made To Henry Mack Half a Century Since," *The Cincinnati Enquirer*, January 24, 1897, 24.
501. Ibid.
502. "Henry Mack's Funeral. The Services Held at the Cemetery Chapel Yesterday Morning," *The Cincinnati Enquirer*, December 28, 1896, 5.
503. "Mack's End," *Cincinnati Post*, December 24, 1896.
504. "Prosit Cincinnati!," *The Cincinnati Enquirer*, May 13, 1976, 6.
505. Louis J. Switchkow and Lloyd P. Gartner, *The History of the Jews of Milwaukee* (Philadelphia: Jewish Publication Society, 1963), 12–23.
506. Harry Barnard, *Julian Mack: The Forging of an American Jew* (New York: Herzl Press, 1974).
507. Sarna and Klein, *Jews of Cincinnati*, 6.
508. "Ralph W. Mack" in *Cincinnati: The Queen City, 1788-1912* by Charles Frederic Goss (Cincinnati: S.J. Clarke, 1912), 776-777.

509. "Walter Staunton Mack" in *Who's Who in America* (Chicago: Marquis Who's Who, Inc., 1970-1971), 1422.
510. "Joseph L. Rauh, Jr." in Ibid., 1861.
511. "Emily S. Rauh" in Ibid.
512. "Harvard Art Museum receives major gift from Emily Rauh Pulitzer," *Harvard Gazette*, October 23, 2008.
513. "In Memoriam: Edward Hirsch Levi, President Emeritus," *The University of Chicago Chronicle* 19, no. 2.
514. John N. Bingham, *Biographical Dictionary of American Business Leaders* (Westport, Connecticut: Greenwood Press, 1983).
515. Pat Garafolo, "Five Years After the Crash," *U.S. News & World Report*, September 14, 2013.
516. Donald L. Miller, *Lewis Mumford: A Life* (New York: Weidenfeld & Nicolson, 1989).
517. Switchkow and Gartner, *Jews of Milwaukee*, loc. cit.
518. Alfred E. Lee, *History of the City of Columbus, Capital of Ohio* (Chicago: Munsell & Co., 1892).
519. Marc Lee Raphael, *Jews and Judaism in a Midwestern Community: Columbus, Ohio, 1840-1975* (Columbus, Ohio: Ohio Historical Society, 1979).
520. Isidor Coons, loc. cit.
521. Marjorie Levin, *Jews of Wilkes-Barre* (Harveys Lake, Pennsylvania: Jewish Community Center of Wyoming Valley, 1999).
522. *The Occident*, October 1848 and October 1849.
523. Isidor Coons, loc. cit.

Index

Adolphus, Lewis, 17
Alexander II (Czar), 38
Allemania Club, 66-67
Altenkunstadt, Bavaria, 11
American Israelite, 31, 71
Americans for Democratic Action, 75
anti-Semitism, 1
   in America, 2, 18, 26-27, 47, 52-53, 65-66, 71, 75, 79
   in Bavaria, 5, 6-7
   in Russia, 38-39
Avondale, Ohio, 68
Bamberg, Bavaria, 3, 5
Bamberger, Babette (née Mack) (aunt), 70
Bamberger, Feiss (uncle), 70
Bene Israel (Cincinnati), 29
Bene Yeshurun (Cincinnati), 29-35, 71
Benjamin, I.J., 65
Bible reading in the public schools, 1, 46
Bishop, Richard M., 62, 63, 67
B'nai B'rith, 66
Bonaparte, Napoleon, 5, 29
Brough, John, 45
Browne, Edward Benjamin Morris, 55-56
Catton, Bruce, 26
Chase, Salmon P., 32
Chattanooga Choo Choo, 62
cholera outbreak of 1849, 12, 30, 34
Cincinnati, New Orleans & Texas Pacific (CNO&TP) Railroad, 62-64
Cincinnati Board of Trade, 47
Cincinnati Board of Transportation, 47
Cincinnati Chamber of Commerce, 63
Cincinnati City Council, 1, 41-44
Cincinnati Commercial Tribune, 49
Cincinnati Courier Company, 49
Cincinnati Daily Enquirer, 49
Cincinnati Enquirer, 26
Cincinnati Jewish Hospital, 34
Cincinnati Music Hall, 47
Cincinnati Post, 73
Cincinnati School Board, 1, 45-47
Cincinnati Southern Railway (CSR), 1, 59-64, 72, Board of Trustees, 59-64
Civil Rights Act of 1964, 76
Civil War, 2, 12-13, 15-21, 25-26, 33, 44-45, 59, 77
Cleveland, Grover, 55, 56, 64
clothing manufacturing, 12-13, 15-17, 18-19, 21-23
Clinton, Bill, 76
Colerain Pike, 68, 69
College Hill, Ohio, 17, 69
Compromise of 1877, 51
Constine, John (cousin), 77
Constine, Lewis, 77
Constine, Loeb (uncle), 70
Counts of Giech, 5
Davis, William, 49
Deborah, Die, 71
Demmelsdorf, Bavaria, 3, 5, 6, 7, 10, 11, 29
Democratic National Convention of 1880, 47
Dennison, William, 16
Dickerson, John, 16, 18
Douglas, Stephen, 41
Dow Law of 1886, 51
Duerbeck, J.G., 17

Dun & Co., 12, 13, 65
Eckstein, David, 26
Ely, Reverend, 9
Erie (steamship) disaster, 10, 13
Exoduster Migration of 1879, 51
False Claims Act, 2, 16
Felicity, Ohio, 11, 12
Ferguson, Edward, 60-62
Ferguson Act, 61
Ford, Gerald, 76
Frankfurt-am-Main, Bavaria, 11
Friedenreich, Faust, 17
Fries, Charles, 17, 62
garbage disposal, 1, 43
General Order No. 11, 25-27, 65
German community of Cincinnati, 9, 29, 31, 32, 49, 51, 66, 71-72, 74
Glaser & Bros., 16, 21
Glen Miller Band, 62
Grant, Jesse, 25, 26, 49
Grant, Ulysses S., 2, 25-27, 49, 50, 51
H.&A. Mack
Hamburg, Germany, 7
Hamilton County Military Committee, 44-45
Harrison, Benjamin, 55-56
Hayes, Rutherford B., 41, 50, 62
Haymarket Square riots, 23
Hebrew Emigration Aid Society (HEAS), 38-39
Hebrew Union College, 32, 38, 45, 67, 71
Hilton, Henry, 65
Home for Incurables, 73
Hooker, Joseph, 45
horsecars, 41-42, 67
Humphrey, Hubert, 75
immigration of Jews
   from Eastern Europe, 38-39
   from Germany, 6-7, 9-10
International Exposition of Textile Fabrics of 1869, 22
Jackson, Ebenezer, Jr., 11
Jergens, 69
Jewish Reform Movement, 1, 29-35, 37-39, 66, 67
Johnson, Andrew, 45
Johnson, Edgar, 46
Judenweg, 5
Krauss family, 10
Kraus, William, 18-19
Ku Klux Klan, 50
Kuhn & Rinskoft, 18
Labold & Newburgh, 53
Lehman, Robert, 76
Lehman Brothers, 76
Levi, Edward Hirsch, 76
Lincoln, Abraham, 15, 26, 41, 44
Lodge Street Synagogue, 30
Lovett, Thomas, 60, 61
McCarthy, Joseph, 75
Mack, Abraham (brother), 5, 6, 9-14, 34, 70, 75
Mack, Alfred (son), 11, 75
Mack, David (brother), 6, 12, 70
Mack, Emil (son), 11, 61, 72
Mack, Esther (née Wolfsheimer) (mother), 3, 5, 11
Mack, Harmon (brother), 5, 7, 12, 21, 22-23, 34, 35, 62, 70
Mack, Harry (son), 11, 69

Mack, Henrietta (daughter), 11, 33, 68, 70
Mack, Henry
  ancestry, 3
  contributions to Bene Yeshurun, 29-35
    Lodge Street Synagogue, 30
    Plum Street (Isaac Mayer Wise) Temple, 33-34
    recruitment of Isaac Mayer Wise, 31-32
    Talmud Yelodim Institute, 30-31
  Benjamin Harrison campaigner, 55-56
  birth, 5
  character
    criticized, 42, 49, 52, 63
    praised, 13, 18, 25, 42, 49, 65
  childhood, 5-6
  as Cincinnati city councilman, 41-44
    promotion of garbage disposal, 43
    promotion of public transportation, 41-42
    promotion of sewage system, 42-43
  as Cincinnati School Board member, 45-47
    favoring Bible reading in the public schools, 46
    Cincinnati Public Library, 45-46
  as Cincinnati Southern Railway trustee, 59-64
    feud with Edward Ferguson, 60-62
    Mack Bill, 63-64
  as clothier, 12-13, 15, 16-17, 18-19, 21-23
    Civil War uniforms manufacturer, 16-19
  death, 73
  friendships
    with Louis Stix, 6, 10
    with Isaac Mayer Wise, 65, 73
  Grant-Mack cotton deal, 25-27, 49, 50
  Hamilton County Military Committee chairman, 44-45
  home in Mt. Airy, 21, 68-70, 73
  immigration to United States, 6-7
  learning English, 9
  marriage to Rosalia Mack, 11
  as Ohio state senator, 51-53, 63-64
    Mack Bill, 63-64
    opposition to Prohibition, 51-53
  peddling, 9, 10-11
  poor health, 55, 56, 73
  move to Cincinnati, 9-10
  physical appearance
    as old man, 72-73
    as young man, 11
  contributions to Reform Judaism, 29-35, 37-39
    Hebrew Union College, 38
    Union of American Hebrew Congregations, 37
  return to Bavaria
    for medical care, 55, 72
    for mother's funeral, 11, 73
Mack, Herman, 75, 76
Mack, Isaac (grandfather), 3, 6-7
Mack, Isaac (nephew), 22, 23
Mack, Isaac (son), 11-12, 34
Mack, Julian, 75
Mack, Julie (sister), 6, 12
Mack, Julius (brother), 6, 12, 70
Mack, Leonard W. (brother-in-law), 17
Mack, Lewis, 75, 76
Mack, Louisa (daughter), 11, 69
Mack, Mannlein (brother), 5
Mack, Mannlein (great grandfather), 3
Mack, Marc (nephew), 22
Mack, Martin (brother), 6, 12, 76
Mack, Millie (daughter), 11, 70
Mack, Moses Isaac (father), 3, 5, 6, 12, 29, 30, 70
Mack, Rosalia (wife), 11, 63, 65, 68, 71, 73, 75
Mack, Seligmann (brother), 6
Mack, Simon (brother), 6, 12, 21, 33, 70, 76
Mack, Theodore (son), 11, 72, 75
Mack, Walter Staunton, 75
Mack, Willie (son), 11-12
Mack & Bros., 12, 13, 16
Mack Bill, 63-64

Mack, Glaser & Co., 21
Mack, Stadler & Co., 21-23, 65, 70
Mack, Stadler & Glaser, 16-19, 21
Madeira, island of, 14
Main River, 5
Marschuetz, Jacob, 44
Marschuetz, Morris J., 44
Masons, 11, 12, 66
Matrikel, 5
May Day strikes, 23
Monroe, Ohio, 11, 12
Mt. Airy, Ohio, 21, 68, 69, 73
Mt. Airy, Venice, and Liberty Railroad, 69-70
Mumford, Charles, 76
National Registry of Historic Places, 33, 47
New York City Metropolitan Museum of Art, 76
New York Times, 14
New York Tribune, 70
Newburgh, Abram (son-in-law), 53, 70
Newburgh, Charles, 69
Newburgh, Henry, 22
Obama, Barack, 76
Occident, 30
Ochs family, 5
Over-the-Rhine neighborhood, 71
Owen Law of 1888, 52-53
Pace, Henry, 21
Panic of 1873, 60
peddling, 6, 9, 10
Pepsicola, 75
Phoenix Club, 66
Plum Street (Isaac Mayer Wise) Temple, 33-34
presidential elections, 2
  of 1868, 26
  of 1876, 50-51
  of 1888, 55-57
Prince of Wales, 43-44
Pritz family, 10
Proctor & Gamble, 21, 69
Pulitzer, Emily Rauh, 76
Pulitzer, Joseph, Jr., 76
Quay, Matthew, 55, 56
Queen and Crescent Route, 62-63
Railroad Strike of 1877, 60
Rauh, Joseph, 75
Reconstruction, end of, 51
Republican National Convention of 1876, 50
Roosevelt, Eleanor, 75
Roosevelt, Franklin Delano, 75
Rosencrans, William, 45
Russell, John, 17
Sauquoit Creek Bridge train wreck, 14
Schutz, 3, 6-7
Select Committee on Government Contracts, 15, 16, 18-19
sewage system, 1, 42-43
sewing machines, 12-13
Sherman, William Tecumseh, 62
shoddy, 2, 15
smallpox outbreak, 22
Springer, Freidenreich & Co., 17
Stadler, Max, 17
Stadler & Bros., 16
Stadler family, 10
Stix, Carl, 10
Stix, Louis, 6, 7, 9-10
Stix family, 10
Straus, Oscar, 56
Sunday laws, 32, 52-53, 66
Taft, Alphonso, 59, 62
Taft, William Howard, 59
Taglicher, 49
Talmud Yelodim Institute, 30-31, 45
Temperance Movement, 2, 51-53
Tilden, Samuel, 50
Tod, David, 44

Touro, Judah, 30
"Trefa Banquet", 67
Union of American Hebrew Congregations (UAHC), 37-38
United Jewish Cemetery, 34
Vajen, John H., 18
Walnut Hills, Ohio, 67-68, 73
Willich, August, 45
Wise, Isaac Mayer, 29, 30, 31, 32, 37, 55, 65, 71, 73
Wise, Julius, 65
Wochen-blatt, 49
Wolfsheimer, Lemel (grandfather), 3
Zion College, 32, 45

About the Author

Born in Cleveland, Ohio, Michael W. Rich graduated with a B.A. from Brown University and an M.D. from the University of Toledo College of Medicine. He currently serves as Associate Professor of Internal Medicine at Northeast Ohio Medical University and core faculty and Interim Chair of the Department of Medicine at Summa Health in Akron, Ohio. Rich lives in Hudson, Ohio with his wife Tina and their children Jacob, Elizabeth, David, and Benjamin.

Apprentice House Press
Loyola University Maryland

Apprentice House is the country's only campus-based, student-staffed book publishing company. Directed by professors and industry professionals, it is a nonprofit activity of the Communication Department at Loyola University Maryland.

Using state-of-the-art technology and an experiential learning model of education, Apprentice House publishes books in untraditional ways. This dual responsibility as publishers and educators creates an unprecedented collaborative environment among faculty and students, while teaching tomorrow's editors, designers, and marketers.

Outside of class, progress on book projects is carried forth by the AH Book Publishing Club, a co-curricular campus organization supported by Loyola University Maryland's Office of Student Activities.

Eclectic and provocative, Apprentice House titles intend to entertain as well as spark dialogue on a variety of topics. Financial contributions to sustain the press's work are welcomed. Contributions are tax deductible to the fullest extent allowed by the IRS.

To learn more about Apprentice House books or to obtain submission guidelines, please visit www.apprenticehouse.com.

Apprentice House
Communication Department
Loyola University Maryland
4501 N. Charles Street
Baltimore, MD 21210
Ph: 410-617-5265 • Fax: 410-617-2198
info@apprenticehouse.com • www.apprenticehouse.com